Times of Refreshing

Ruth Gregg

O&U

Onwards & Upwards

Onwards and Upwards Publishers

3 Radfords Turf, Cranbrook, Exeter,
EX5 7DX, United Kingdom.
www.onwardsandupwards.org

First edition, published in the United Kingdom by Onwards and Upwards Publishers (2019).

ISBN: 978-1-78815-536-6
Typeface: Sabon LT
Graphic design: LM Graphic Design

Every effort has been made by the author to obtain the necessary permissions to reproduce copyrighted material. If, however, there have been any omissions or errors, please contact the publisher to have these corrected in future reprints and editions.

The views and opinions expressed in this book are the author's own, and do not necessarily represent the views and opinions of Onwards and Upwards Publishers or its staff.

Endorsements

Times of Refreshing does what it says on the tin – it is full to overflowing with spiritual refreshment. At a time when spiritual attentiveness and soul care can be such easily neglected spiritual disciplines, due to the busy demands made on our lives by so many other things, this spiritually anointed and biblically literate gem of Ruth's is pure gold. It is a collection of inspiring and deeply personal devotionals which come out of a heart which has been captivated by the Father's amazing love and longs for deep personal and national revival – you will certainly meet the Saviour in its pages.

Rev. Daniel Kane
West Presbyterian Church, Ballymena

There are often times in the normal day-to-day hectic schedule of ministry life that you run out of steam and need to have a pit-stop. Sadly, I am on first name terms with a lot of the deli-counter staff and hot food staff all over Ballymena! This also can be said of our walk with God; we can run out of steam and need a pit-stop. In *Times of Refreshing*, Ruth has provided the perfect spiritual pick-me-up – a devotional that can allow us to pause, rest for a while, have a spiritual snack and recharge our batteries. Better than any meal deal, *Times of Refreshing* will help us run our race and fight our battles. In fact, why don't you get your copy and keep it where you work and make it part of your daily pit-stop routine? Ruth, thank you for this gift. My prayer, like yours, is that many will find essential daily spiritual refreshing as they use *Times of Refreshing*.

Rev. Mark McConnell
Rector, Ballymena Parish Church

There is nothing quite as good for any of us as to spend the first part of the day meditating on the Word of God. As I have read through this beautiful devotional that Ruth has written, I know that many lives will be refreshed and encouraged. Ruth has brought fresh revelation on the Scriptures and nuggets of truth that you can ponder on throughout the day. I highly recommend this book as a tool for anyone who hungers for more of God.

Pastor Roy Stewart
Pastor, Celebration House, Ballymena

About the Author

 Ruth has been involved in ministry for the past 30 years. She holds a B.D. from Queens University, a Doctorate in Biblical Studies from CLU, has released various print publications, and currently resides in County Antrim, Northern Ireland. She is director of Impact Unlimited Bible College and CTTW, a 24/7 global prayer initiative.

Her passion is to inspire others through writing in a way that is insightful, meaningful and relevant. In the *Times of Refreshing* devotionals, she taps into her experiences as a pastor, teacher, wife and mother of two, to relate poignant stories from real-life experiences.

To contact the author, please write to:

Ruth Gregg
c/o Onwards and Upwards Publishers Ltd.
3 Radfords Turf
Exeter
EX5 7DX

More information about the author can be found at:

www.onwardsandupwards.org/ruth-gregg

Foreword by Tommy Stewart

Times of Refreshing is a devotional full of life-changing words of inspiration and encouragement written by Dr Ruth Gregg, drawn from a lifetime of study of God's Word. The devotional has been written to encourage the reader to trust God in every circumstance of life and to give the reader courage each day to step out in faith, believing that God is with them and has good plans for their lives.

I have known Dr Ruth Gregg from our college days when Ruth was studying Theology and I was studying Economics. My earliest impressions were of someone deeply committed to the study of God's Word and to being able to communicate it in such a way that the Word of God came alive in the life of the hearer. Through Ruth's ministry, both as a pastor and a teacher, she has shown herself to be "a worker who does not need to be ashamed and who correctly handles the Word of truth" (2 Tim. 2:15). Her dedication to creating teaching materials for pastors in the 10/40 window and her passion for revival mean that Ruth's writings are filled with great truths, anointed by the Holy Spirit.

If, like me, you have struggled to read and meditate daily on what the Bible has to say, then *Times of Refreshing* will provide you with the opportunity to develop a daily rhythm of reading and meditating on the truth of God's Word.

It is said that it takes twenty-one days to develop a habit. I can think of few better habits that you could develop than creating space each day, with the help of *Times of Refreshing*, to be refreshed by God's Word.

I wonder, can you answer yes to any of the following questions?

- Do you want to have a deeper sense of God's peace?
- Do you want to grow closer to God?
- Do you want to be more like Jesus?
- Do you want to know more of God's Word?
- Do you want to grow in confidence in who you are in Christ?

Then, be assured, *Times of Refreshing* is for you!

Tommy Stewart
Founder/Director, Christians Who Lead

December

December

1

Through the Roof

And they came, bringing to Him a paralytic, carried by four men. And being unable to get to Him because of the crowd, they removed the roof above Him; and when they had dug an opening, they let down the pallet on which the paralytic was lying. And Jesus seeing their faith said to the paralytic, "Son, your sins are forgiven."

Mark 2:3-5 (NASB)

e use the idiom 'through the roof' to imply that something has suddenly rocketed in price, seemingly out of control. The price of petrol, taxes, the crime rate and even tempers can all go 'through the roof'. In Mark 2:1-12 we see a man literally go through the roof, thanks to his four faithful friends. Jesus was in a house, teaching a large group of people. The place was packed.

Verses 3 and 4 tell us of four faithful friends – friends who cared enough to be inconvenienced for another. They could have said, *he's too heavy, we've left it too late, the crowd is too large, maybe we'll try next time Jesus is in town.* They could have said, *we've never done anything like this before; what will people think?* They could have gone home discouraged and missed the miracle, but thankfully they refused to quit. I love people who think outside the box, people with unlimited vision, people with a can-do attitude. These four friends removed the lid of human limitation.

Can you think of a friend you could help today? What action is needed? What kind of friend are you? We are told that iron sharpens iron.

As iron sharpens iron,
So a man sharpens the countenance of his friend...

Proverbs 27:17 (NKJV)

When iron blades are rubbed together, each becomes sharper and thus more effective. Likewise, when believers are involved in one another's lives, mutual edification occurs. This scripture emphasises the importance of making friends with quality people who help to improve us. Do you have other 'irons' in your life who can help in sharpening you? Do you have friends who are willing to lift you up to Jesus? Just like the paralysed man, we are dependent on the grace and compassion of those around us; and like the four friends, we need friends whose faith is active. Not only was their faith active but their actions showed that they were convinced that Jesus could do something for their friend.

What can God do with four faithful and faith-filled friends? Read the story of Daniel, Shadrach, Meshach and Abednego, and how together they took their stand for God.[1] Read church history and you will see how Rev. J. H. Moore exhorted young men in a Bible class to "Do something more for God." Four faithful friends – James McQuilkin, Jeremiah Meneely, Robert Carlisle and John Wallace – responded by gathering for prayer at Tawnybrack Old Sabbath School in Kells, Northern Ireland, prior to the 1859 revival. As they read and meditated upon the Scripture, their hearts began to burn with an unquenchable fire from heaven, which set all Ulster ablaze for God. A little pillar marks the site today and says:

> *Behind this pillar was the location of fervent prayer meetings before the 1859 revival.*

---

[1] See Daniel 1:6-21

2

The Next Generation

We will not hide these truths from our children;
*   we will tell the next generation*
about the glorious deeds of the LORD,
*   about his power and his mighty wonders.*

Psalm 78:4 (NLT)

*I*t seems as if every family has its own traditions, whether they make sense or not. We imitate and treasure the things we learn from our parents, and we pass on those same traditions, ideals and values to our own children. If something is important to us, we naturally want to share it with our children. But what is the most important thing we can hand down to the next generation? The psalmist says:

...we will tell the next generation the praiseworthy deeds of the
LORD, his power, and the wonders he has done ... to teach their
children, so that the next generation would know them ... and
they in turn would tell their children. Then they would put their
trust in God...

Psalm 78:4-7 (NIVUK)

Who's responsible for telling the next generation? " *We* will not hide these truths." We must assist in the preservation and transmission of all God's revelation to the next generation. The verb "hide" in this verse has a very specific meaning. It means to keep something back, to refuse to make something known. When someone was asked to report something, they were often charged "not to hide anything", similar to asking someone to tell the truth, the whole truth and nothing but the truth today.[2]

---

[2] See Joshua with Achan in Joshua 7:19; Eli with Samuel in 1 Samuel 3:17

Share with them God's mighty deeds recorded in the Bible. Share with them about men and women whom God has used mightily throughout history. Check out some good biographies at the Christian bookshop. Share with them personal stories of how God has answered prayer in your life. Let them see the impact God has on your faith in everyday struggles and trials. Most of all, share with them what God has done through the sending of his Son Jesus to bring us salvation.

> *Let each generation tell its children of your mighty acts; let them proclaim your power.*
>
> *Psalm 145:4 (NLT)*

> *...so the next generation might know them – even the children not yet born – and they in turn will teach their own children.*
>
> *Psalm 78:6 (NLT)*

Joshua learned a great deal from Moses and his generation, leaving behind this wonderful statement:

> *As for me and my household, we will serve the LORD.*
>
> *Joshua 24:15 (NIV)*

But the very next generation was described as one which knew neither the Lord nor what he had done for Israel.[3] Karl Marx said that to conquer a nation you just have to block the transfer of values, morals and beliefs between generations. May we do our part to transmit God's truth.

> *...we will tell the next generation about the glorious deeds of the LORD, about his power and his mighty wonders.*
>
> *Psalm 78:4 (NLT)*

---

[3] See Judges 2:10

3

Burnt Stones

Now it came about that when Sanballat heard that we were rebuilding the wall, he became furious and very angry and mocked the Jews. He spoke in the presence of his brothers and the wealthy men of Samaria and said, "What are these feeble Jews doing? Are they going to restore it for themselves? Can they offer sacrifices? Can they finish in a day? Can they revive the stones from the dusty rubble even the burnt ones?"

Nehemiah 4:1-2 (NASB)

When Nehemiah came to Jerusalem to rebuild the walls of the city, he was mocked by Sanballat, the Horonite. Nehemiah 4:2 records the voice of the enemy:

"Will they revive the stones from the heaps of rubbish – stones that are burned?"

Nehemiah 4:2 (NKJV)

Today the enemy of the work of God is making the same railing accusations, seeking to discourage and demoralise. Both the rebuilt temple and the walls of the city were constructed with stones that had been burnt during the destruction of the former temple and city. These were the ones that had been through the previous failure and now looked useless for building anything, much less the glorious temple of the Lord or the walls of Jerusalem. But every one of them had a place in the plan of God.

Are you one of the burnt stones? Are you charred and marred, burnt by religion, burnt by failure, burnt by past relationships, burnt by disappointments? Have you been through a work that seemed glorious and pregnant with potential, only to see it end in a terrible disappointment? If so, then you are a prime candidate for the glorious new work that the Lord is doing today. The stones Nehemiah used had been pulled out of position, removed out of the wall of destiny, out of

13

where God has positioned them. They had been through the fire – they had been tested. God's got a plan for burnt stones. His plan is to revive them and restore them, to get them back in position again and give them significance and purpose.

The enemy would have us to believe that it's useless, it's hopeless, that all our efforts are in vain. *You're a nobody, you're rubbish, you're trash, you're good for nothing, nobody wants you.* You can hear the scorn, derision and sarcasm in the comments of Sanballat, "Can they revive the stones from the dusty rubble even the burnt ones?" God's answer is a resounding yes. The wall was rebuilt with the stones which were burnt.

Maybe today you are thinking, *can I ever rise up out of this mess; can I ever find a place where I fit; can God ever use me again?* Nehemiah used the burnt and charred stones to fortify a city. Encourage someone today with the good news that God can restore a burnt stone and set it back in its place in the wall of His plan and purpose, and from a charred mess the embers can be rekindled and become a flame ablaze with His glory.

4

What Do You See?

I will stand at my watch and station myself on the ramparts; I will look to see what he will say to me...

Habakkuk 2:1 (NIV)

People sometimes share a picture and ask you, "What do you see?" Some people see a vase in the picture; others immediately see the face of a person. Usually if you stare at it long enough you can see both. The song *What a Wonderful World* starts with the words, "I see trees of green, red roses too. I see them bloom for me and you. And I think to myself, what a wonderful world." In the Bible God asks people, "What do you see?" One such person was Jeremiah.

The word of the LORD came to me: "What do you see, Jeremiah?" "I see the branch of an almond tree," I replied. ... And the word of the LORD came to me the second time, saying, "What do you see?" And I said, "I see a boiling pot, facing away from the north."

Jeremiah 1:11,13 (NIV)

Amos was asked the same question.

And the LORD said to me, "Amos, what do you see?" And I said, A plumb line." ... And he said, "What do you see, Amos?" And I said, "A basket of summer fruit."

Amos 7:8; 8:2 (ESV)

Zechariah 4:2 records another example:

And said to me, "What do you see?" I said, "I see, and behold, a lampstand all of gold with its bowl on the top of it, and its seven lamps on it with seven spouts belonging to each of the lamps which are on the top of it."

Zechariah 4:2 (ESV)

What do you see in the Spirit? What is God showing you? I see a generation arising who seek God as their vital necessity and know their God and are ready for great exploits in His Name. I see a people adopting the posture of prayer. I see mindsets being transformed by the Word of God. I see the people of God awakening to the fresh revelation of who they really are in Christ, who Christ is in them and the authority that they possess in His Name. I see dry bones coming together, God breathing life into them and an exceedingly great army rising up, getting into alignment for their assignment. I see yokes being destroyed because of the anointing, burdens being lifted off people's shoulders, chains being broken, captives being set free. I see doors of opportunity opening in unprecedented ways for the gospel, doors which no-one can shut. I see God making a way in the wilderness and rivers in the desert. I see wells being unblocked and unstopped. I see revival, a fresh wind and wave of God's glory that is about to sweep the nations, ushering in an un-countable harvest of souls.

Take time to allow God to show you His heart, to see life from His perspective. As you look into His Word, ask Him to open your eyes to behold His wondrous truths.

I will stand at my watch and station myself on the ramparts; I will look to see what he will say to me...

Habakkuk 2:1 (NIV)

May the eyes of our hearts be enlightened, as Paul prayed:

I pray that the eyes of your heart may be enlightened in order that you may know the hope to which he has called you, the riches of his glorious inheritance in his holy people, and his incomparably great power for us who believe.

Ephesians 1:18-19 (NIV)

5

Holy Plans

Before I formed you in the womb I knew you; before you were born I sanctified you; I ordained you a prophet to the nations.

Jeremiah 1:5 (NKJV)

I sanctified you. I separated you and set you apart. Before you saw the light of day, I had holy plans for you. Paul introduced himself in Romans by saying:

Paul, a bondservant of Jesus Christ, called to be an apostle, separated to the gospel of God.

Romans 1:1 (NKJV)

He was separated to the gospel of God. The word he used for "separated" is *aphorizo,* meaning 'to set apart for purpose' or 'mark off with boundaries'. He used the word again in Galatians:

...God, who had set me apart even from my mother's womb and called me through His grace...

Galatians 1:15 (NASB)

Both Jeremiah and Paul knew that God had holy plans for them. In Ephesians 2 Paul is writing to the church at Ephesus and says:

For we are his workmanship, created in Christ Jesus for good works, which God prepared beforehand, that we should walk in them.

Ephesians 2:10 (ESV)

The expression in Jeremiah 1:5, "I formed you", has the nuance of a potter's care and expertise, a theme Jeremiah will later expound in chapter eighteen. Jeremiah is being told, "I formed you like a pot. You are hand-made and uniquely formed for the task. You are a bespoke work of art – individually crafted." We too can rest in the same truth that God has holy plans for us. He shaped us in advance for those plans, wired us for our assignment. The Bible declares that God created each of us with a special, positive purpose. Whatever job we do, it is a holy calling, a sacred calling, a responsibility given to us by God to serve Him there. It is an opportunity to be shining lights of integrity, dedication, humility, service and love. Pay attention to how He has gifted you. His plan for you will always be directly related to the gifts that He has bestowed upon you.

When Jeremiah was given his job, he looked for a way out, claiming that he wasn't a good speaker and that he was much too young. Many of us give excuses as well when we're given a tough task. But God had equipped him for his purpose and promised to be with him. He said:

> *"I'll tell you where to go and you'll go there.*
> *I'll tell you what to say and you'll say it.*
> *Don't be afraid of a soul.*
> *I'll be right there, looking after you."*

Jeremiah 1:7-8 (MSG)

It's time to align yourself with God's purpose and His will for your life. Get in alignment for your God-given assignment. Don't delay – the destinies of people and nations may be depending on it.

6

Say No to Ono

Sanballat and Geshem sent to me, saying, Come, let us meet together in one of the villages in the plain of Ono. But they intended to do me harm. And I sent messengers to them, saying, I am doing a great work and cannot come down. Why should the work stop while I leave to come down to you? They sent to me four times this way, and I answered them as before.

Nehemiah 6:2-4 (AMPC)

Nehemiah was called by God to go to Jerusalem and lead the people to rebuild the broken down walls of the city. It was an important, God-directed, God-sized task. As such, it incurred the wrath and opposition of the enemy as he tried every possible way to derail the project, discourage the builders and defeat the Lord's plans. On one occasion, the enemies of God tried to lure Nehemiah away from the rebuilding of the wall by asking for a conference to discuss their differences. They wanted him to take a break from the building and meet them at the plains of Ono. Nehemiah could see through their deception and said, "Oh, no," to Ono. He told them he was doing a great work and could not come down to meet them. I love that. Nehemiah valued the work that God had called him to perform. He called it a "great work". He saw that what he was doing – an unglamorous, dusty, backbreaking job – was in reality a great work for God. Any God-directed work is a great work and Nehemiah refused to be distracted from it.

"I am doing a great work and cannot come down." This is a great verse for us all to embrace. It is one which I have underlined, circled, asterisked and underlined again! It focuses our attention aright, exercising wisdom and discernment. We are all carrying out the Great Commission and must press ahead. We cannot allow ourselves to be distracted.

Let your eyes look right on [with fixed purpose], and let your gaze be straight before you. Consider well the path of your feet, and let all your ways be established and ordered aright. Turn not aside to the right hand or to the left; remove your foot from evil.

Proverbs 4:25-27 (AMPC)

Keep your eyes straight ahead; ignore all sideshow distractions. Watch your step, and the road will stretch out smooth before you. Look neither right nor left; leave evil in the dust.

Proverbs 4:25-27 (MSG)

Our focus is Jesus.

...fixing our eyes on Jesus, the pioneer and perfecter of faith.

Hebrews 12:2 (NIV)

Notice when the distraction came to Nehemiah. The workers were just days away from seeing the vision completed.

I had rebuilt the wall and not a gap was left in it – though up to that time I had not set the doors in the gates...

Nehemiah 6:1 (NIV)

Nehemiah was at a very dangerous time. When the novelty of the vision has worn off, the people are weary and you're almost done, it's easy to get distracted. Four times they sent Nehemiah the same message and four times he sent the same answer. Every day of our lives, opportunities have a way of coming up that have the potential to distract us from the main things that God has called us to do. We need to be alert and recognise them as distractions. Peter told us:

Be alert and of sober mind. Your enemy the devil prowls around like a roaring lion looking for someone to devour. Resist him, standing firm in the faith, because you know that the family of believers throughout the world is undergoing the same kind of sufferings.

1 Peter 5:8-9 (NIV)

Do we have the courage and determination to say, "Oh, no"?

7

He Who Has an Ear, Let Him Hear

He who has an ear, let him hear what the Spirit says to the churches.

Revelation 2:11 (ESV)

*D*o you have an ear to hear? At the end of each of the seven letters to the seven churches[4] is the command, "He who has an ear, let him hear what the Spirit says to the churches." Have you created uninterrupted space in your life to simply be still and quiet before God, listening for His voice speaking into your heart? Take hold of your Bible and instead of breezing through the reading as if you were reading a novel or textbook, read it deliberately and ponder every word. Ask God to reveal specifically what He is saying through that word to you.

Radio and television stations transmit twenty-four hours a day, seven days a week; but we only hear them when we turn the receiver on and tune in. Failure to hear the signal doesn't mean the station isn't transmitting. Likewise, God is constantly transmitting His voice to His sheep, but few are tuned in. Jesus urges us to listen to Him.

"My sheep recognize my voice, and I know them, and they follow me."

John 10:27 (TLB)

When my husband rings me, or my mother or someone else in my family, I immediately know their voice. I don't have to ask who is speaking. I have spent quality time with them each day and recognise their voice straightaway. The same is true when it comes to our relationship with God. We are told:

...faith comes from hearing, and hearing by the word of God.

Romans 10:17 (NKJV)

---

[4] Revelation 2 and 3

God will lead us but we must listen.

And your ears shall hear a word behind you, saying, "This is the way, walk in it," when you turn to the right or when you turn to the left.

Isaiah 30:21 (ESV)

Paul warned Timothy that some people will turn their ears away from the truth:

For the time is coming when people will not endure sound teaching, but having itching ears they will accumulate for themselves teachers to suit their own passions, and will turn away from listening to the truth and wander off into myths.

2 Timothy 4:3-4 (ESV)

Jesus said:

"For this people's heart has grown dull, and with their ears they can barely hear, and their eyes they have closed, lest they should see with their eyes and hear with their ears and understand with their heart and turn, and I would heal them."

Matthew 13:15 (ESV)

Zechariah 7:11 states:

But they refused to pay attention and turned a stubborn shoulder and stopped their ears that they might not hear.

Zechariah 7:11 (ESV)

Stephen told the people:

"You stiff-necked people, uncircumcised in heart and ears, you always resist the Holy Spirit. As your fathers did, so do you."

Acts 7:51 (ESV)

Itching ears which only listen to what suits us; ears which can barely hear; ears which are stopped; what a travesty when we could be tuning into God's frequency and availing of the abundant life He has in store for us. Frances R. Havergal penned the words:

Lord, speak to me, that I may speak in living echoes of thy tone.

That simple line of an old hymn makes a great prayer. May God give us eyes to see, ears to hear and hearts to understand and obey what He reveals.

8

A Brook of Blessing

He gives to them a brook of blessing
filled from the rain of an outpouring.
They grow stronger and stronger with every step forward...

Psalm 84:6b-7 (TPT)

*I*n the previous verse the Psalmist has mentioned "passing through the valley of Baca"[5]. "Baca" means 'tears' but the good news is that we are "passing through". We pass through valleys; we do not live in them. If you are presently in a season of weeping, God will bring you through. David said:

Even though I walk
through the darkest valley,
I will fear no evil...

Psalm 23:4 (NIV)

He divided the sea and led them through;
he made the water stand up like a wall.

Psalm 78:13 (NIV)

...he led them like sheep through the wilderness.

Psalm 78:52 (NIV)

Isaiah prophesied:

When you pass through the waters,
I will be with you;
and when you pass through the rivers,
they will not sweep over you.
When you walk through the fire,

---

[5] NASB

> *you will not be burned;*
> *the flames will not set you ablaze.*

Isaiah 43:2 (NIV)

Note the repetition of the word "through". If you are in a valley of weeping, see yourself coming through and out stronger.

> *Weeping may last for the night,*
> *But a shout of joy comes in the morning.*

Psalm 30:5 (NASB)

The valley of tears is temporary, and look what lies in store: "He gives to them a brook of blessing filled from the rain of an outpouring."

Refreshing rain is coming. In the Bible, rain usually speaks of blessings. In Ezekiel 34:26, God is speaking and He says:

> *I will make them and the places all around My hill a blessing. And I will cause showers to come down in their season; there shall be showers of blessing.*

Ezekiel 34:26 (NASB)

This word "shower" in the Hebrew is *geshem*, which means 'to rain violently, pour down in heavy shower'. God wants to rain blessings in your life – and not just a light rain of blessings. He wants to pour down heavy showers of blessings on you.

> *For I will pour water on him who is thirsty,*
> *And floods on the dry ground;*
> *I will pour My Spirit on your descendants,*
> *And My blessing on your offspring.*

Isaiah 44:3 (NKJV)

This scripture formed the prayer of God's people prior to the Hebrides revival: "Pour water on the thirsty and floods on the dry ground." Are you thirsty? Could you benefit from "a brook of blessing filled from the rain of an outpouring"? Every dry, arid and parched part of your life can be refreshed by God. As the Psalmist said:

> *You gave abundant showers, O God;*
> *you refreshed your weary inheritance.*

Psalm 68:9 (NIV)

Needing strength? Psalm 84:7 goes on to say, "They grow stronger and stronger with every step forward..." or in other words:

They go from strength to strength [increasing in victorious power].

Psalm 84:7 (AMP)

God puts supernatural strength into every stride of faith we take. I love what Habakkuk said when life was difficult:

Though the fig tree does not blossom and there is no fruit on the vines, [though] the product of the olive fails and the fields yield no food, though the flock is cut off from the fold and there are no cattle in the stalls, yet I will rejoice in the Lord; I will exult in the [victorious] God of my salvation! The Lord God is my Strength, my personal bravery, and my invincible army; He makes my feet like hinds' feet and will make me to walk [not to stand still in terror, but to walk] and make [spiritual] progress upon my high places [of trouble, suffering, or responsibility]!

Habakkuk 3:17-19 (AMP)

May God give to us a brook of blessing filled from the rain of His outpouring. May we grow stronger and stronger with every step forward.

9

A 50:20 Perspective

And we know that in all things God works for the good of those who love him, who have been called according to his purpose.

Romans 8:28 (NIV)

I sat down at a table and I sipped my coffee. I remarked, "This is good!" What did I mean? What was so good? Was it the machine which made it? Was it the quality of the water which was part of it? Was it the quality of the coffee beans? Was it the barista who served it with a smile? Was it the cup in which it was served? Was it the ambience of the coffee shop in which I ordered it? Or was it the fact that I was ready for it? The answer is that it was a combination of all of the above. It was the collective cooperation of each element.

So we are convinced that every detail of our lives is continually woven together to fit into God's perfect plan of bringing good into our lives, for we are his lovers who have been called to fulfil his designed purpose.

Romans 8:28 (TPT)

Paul says "all things". All things are under God's control and direction. We will not always understand how all the things we experience work for good, and we certainly will not always enjoy them. But we do know that nothing comes into our lives that God cannot use for His purposes. Paul used the Greek word *sunergeo* which refers to the working together of various elements to produce an effect greater than, and often completely different from, the sum of each element acting separately.

Remember Joseph in the Old Testament? The story goes like this: Joseph's brothers were jealous of him, so they sold him to some traders who took him to Egypt. In Egypt, Joseph was sold into the household of Potiphar, who managed Pharaoh's household. Potiphar was impressed with Joseph and put him in charge, and even grew very fond of him. But

Potiphar's wife wanted to seduce Joseph. Joseph refused her advances, so she framed him for attempted rape, and Potiphar threw Joseph in prison. He spent the better part of his twenties in an Egyptian dungeon, separated from his father, not knowing if he would ever see him again. But in that exact dungeon he was again successful. The warden liked him so much that he put Joseph in charge of the whole operation. And in that exact dungeon Joseph met Pharaoh's head baker and Pharaoh's cupbearer. His successful interpretation of their dreams led Joseph to Pharaoh. And when Joseph interpreted Pharaoh's dream, he was put in control of the kingdom. As Joseph reminisced on his life, he could say to his brothers:

You intended to harm me, but God intended it for good to accomplish what is now being done, the saving of many lives.

Genesis 50:20 (NIV)

Even the trial of the famine was being used to reunite Jacob with his beloved Joseph and to provide for all his needs for the rest of his life. In commenting on Genesis 50:20, Dr. David Seamonds, a Methodist pastor, writes, "All of us need a 50:20 perspective on life." The 50:20 perspective will promote you and position you to bless others. Realise that in all things God works for the good of those who love Him.

10

The Future is Bright

*Not a word failed of any good thing which the LORD had spoken
to the house of Israel. All came to pass.*

Joshua 21:45 (NKJV)

doniram Judson, the great missionary to Burma, stated, "The
future is as bright as the promises of God." Have you ever been
disappointed when someone made a promise to you and failed
to keep it? I imagine we all have felt that way. We live in a world of
broken promises, don't we? From outlandish political promises to over-
the-top ads, many of us have become sceptical whenever we hear
someone make a claim that appears too good to be true. Because of the
disappointment of unfulfilled promises, many place little faith when a
person makes a promise to them. However, God's promises are not like
man's promises. God keeps His promises. God never over-promises and
He never under-delivers.

Notice the passage from Joshua says that "not *a word* failed … *All*
came to pass."[6] God's word is trustworthy. His promises are true. What
God says He will do.

*God is not a man, so he does not lie. He is not human, so he does
not change his mind. Has he ever spoken and failed to act? Has
he ever promised and not carried it through?*

Numbers 23:19 (NLT)

Fast forward into the New Testament. Peter said that God has
"...given to us exceedingly great and precious promises..."[7]

*For all the promises of God find their Yes in him. That is why it
is through him that we utter our Amen to God for his glory.*

2 Corinthians 1:20 (ESV)

---

[6] emphasis added
[7] 2 Peter 1:4 (NKJV)

Are we uttering amen to His promises or are we accepting defeat every day of our lives? Why should we feel alone when God has said, "I will never leave you nor forsake you?" Why accept mediocrity when God has told us we are "more than conquerors"[8] through Christ? Why succumb to the pressures of life when He has said "...my peace I give you. ... Do not let your hearts be troubled and do not be afraid."[9] Why keep saying "I can't" when He says you "can do all things through Christ who strengthens"[10] you? Why give in to condemnation when He says, "...there is now no condemnation for those who are in Christ Jesus"[11]?

We need to apply the promises to our lives. No matter what your circumstance, God's Word has a promise of hope waiting for you. God made a promise to Abraham that he would become the father of many nations. We are told in Romans 4 that Abraham believed the promise and expected God to fulfil it. He took God at His word, and as a result he became the father of many nations.

We need to believe the promises of God which He shares with us in His Word. We need to expect God to fulfil them in our lives. We need to take God at His Word and then we will see the results. Charles Spurgeon once said:

> Do not treat God's promises as if they were curiosities for a museum; but believe them and use them.

By the exercise of our faith, God's promises become personal.

---

[8] Romans 8:37 (NKJV)
[9] John 14:27 (ESV)
[10] Philippians 4:13 (NRSV)
[11] Romans 8:1 (NIV)

11

An Ear for the Weary

The LORD GOD has given Me
The tongue of the learned,
That I should know how to speak
A word in season to him who is weary.
He awakens Me morning by morning,
He awakens My ear
To hear as the learned.

Isaiah 50:4 (NKJV)

The Sovereign LORD has given me a well-instructed tongue, to know the word that sustains the weary. He wakens me morning by morning, wakens my ear to listen like one being instructed.

Isaiah 50:4 (NIV)

The original Hebrew reads, "...that I might know how to strengthen with a word the weary." In the Gospels we see how our Lord had "a word in season to him who is weary". He encouraged all who were weary to come to Him and rest. Matthew 11:28-29 records His very words:

"Come to me, all you who are weary and burdened, and I will give you rest. Take my yoke upon you and learn from me, for I am gentle and humble in heart, and you will find rest for your souls."

Matthew 11:28-29 (NIV)

Jesus had the right word to speak into every situation, a "well-instructed tongue", and He has left us an example of how to minister to people who have grown weary. He wants us to have an instructed word to sustain those who have been beaten down by life through rejection, fear, disappointment and disillusionment. Do you know someone who needs a timely word of encouragement?

Ask God to help you to:

- *speak the right word* – a well-instructed tongue which knows the right a word to share;
- *speak at the right time* – in season (*kairos*);
- *speak to the right person* – to him who is weary.

Have you an 'ear' to hear a word for the weary? How do we get this word? Isaiah says, "He wakens me morning by morning, wakens my ear to listen like one being instructed." Notice the words "morning by morning" – on a daily basis. This makes our lives so exciting. We simply have to listen like one being instructed.

I often think of the maid in Naaman's household whose word in season led him to travel to Israel to receive his miraculous healing from leprosy.

> *Now bands ... from Aram had gone out and had taken captive a young girl from Israel, and she served Naaman's wife. She said to her mistress, "If only my master would see the prophet who is in Samaria! He would cure him of his leprosy."*
>
> *2 Kings 5:2-3 (NIV)*

How carefully she spoke it and yet with such assurance. Proverbs tells us:

> *A man hath joy by the answer of his mouth: and a word spoken in due season how good is it!*
>
> *Proverbs 15:23 (KJV)*

> *A word fitly spoken is like apples of gold in pictures of silver.*
>
> *Proverbs 25:11 (KJV)*

A word of comfort to the weary can go a long way.

12

P, D, N or R?

Yet they did not obey or incline their ear, but followed the counsels and the dictates of their evil hearts, and went backward and not forward.

Jeremiah 7:24 (NKJV)

A number of cars come with automatic transmissions. My car is manual but inside my mother's car, an automatic, you will see the letters P, D, N and R — Park, Drive (forward), Neutral and Reverse. 'Park' mechanically locks the transmission, restricting the car from moving in any direction. 'Drive' is the proper setting for those wanting to make efficient progress and accelerate through the gears. 'Neutral' means that we aren't active or moving. 'Reverse' means that we are backing up or going backward.

Look at what God says in this amazing scripture:

"But this is what I commanded them, saying, 'Obey My voice, and I will be your God, and you will be My people; and you will walk in all the way which I command you, that it may be well with you.' Yet they did not obey or incline their ear, but walked in their own counsels and in the stubbornness of their evil heart, and went backward and not forward."

Jeremiah 7:23-24 (NASB)

How much clearer can God be? When we listen to His voice, we will go forward, make progress and grow. When we don't listen, we will go backward, lose progress and fail. For the believer who desires to grow, there is absolutely nothing more important in this life than to hear His voice and heed it. The Amplified Bible phrases it:

But this thing I did command them: Listen to and obey My voice, and I will be your God and you will be My people; and walk in the whole way that I command you, that it may be well with you. But they would not listen to and obey Me or bend their ear [to

Me], but followed the counsels and the stubborn promptings of their own evil hearts and minds, and they turned their backs and went in reverse instead of forward.

Jeremiah 7:23-24 (AMP)

They went in Reverse, but Drive (forward) is the appropriate setting for those wanting to make progress. Moses was instructed by the Lord:

"Tell the people of Israel to go forward."

Exodus 14:15 (ESV)

To go forward we must listen to the voice of God and walk in the way He instructs. God said:

But My people would not heed My voice,
And Israel would have none of Me.
So I gave them over to their own stubborn heart,
To walk in their own counsels.
"Oh, that My people would listen to Me,
that Israel would walk in My ways!"

Psalm 81:11-13 (NKJV)

When you listen to His voice, you will go forward, make progress, prosper and grow. God has great things in store for you. Do not settle for where you are but get ready for the next level. It is time to shift gears and see some growth and transformation. You have a destiny to take hold of. Paul said:

Not that I have already obtained it or have already become perfect, but I press on so that I may lay hold of that for which also I was laid hold of by Christ Jesus. Brethren, I do not regard myself as having laid hold of it yet; but one thing I do: forgetting what lies behind and reaching forward to what lies ahead, I press on toward the goal for the prize of the upward call of God in Christ Jesus.

Philippians 3:12-14 (NASB)

In Deuteronomy God says:

"You have stayed long enough at this mountain. Break camp and advance..."

Deuteronomy 1:6-7 (NIV)

To go forward and advance you too must listen to the voice of God and walk in the way He instructs. Only then will you ever experience the greater things that God has planned for you.

13

If You Knew the Gift

Jesus answered her, "If you knew the gift of God and who it is that asks you for a drink, you would have asked him and he would have given you living water."

John 4:10 (NIV)

A lady wanted to buy some Christmas gifts for her special friends. In the busy weeks before Christmas, time ran out and she had to abandon her idea of buying gifts. She decided instead to send each friend a Christmas card. It would be much cheaper and easier. She was very pleased to find a pack of 50 cards. She liked the picture on the front. "That's perfect," she thought to herself. Once home she quickly signed all the cards, "With all my love," and mailed them to her friends. Two weeks later, after New Year, she happened to look more carefully at one of the leftover cards from that pack of 50. She was shocked to read the printed message inside the card, which obviously she had not noticed before. It said, "This Christmas card is just to say, a little gift is on its way."

Christmas is the season for giving gifts but giving the perfect gift is difficult. It's hard to pinpoint a person's taste and what they need in their life and match it to your gifting budget and keep it appropriate for your relationship. Choosing the right Christmas gift can be a minefield and may even cause apprehension and anxiety for some.

According to an online source, there are two strategies for finding the right gift. The first is to be 'recipient-centric' – where you try to find a gift that reflects the qualities or interests of the person receiving the gift. The second is to be 'giver-centric' – which is where you are focused on giving something that reflects your own personality or discloses something about you as an individual. We all try to find that 'perfect gift'. We know God gave mankind the Perfect Gift when He sent His Son Jesus. Jesus reflects the One who gave Him and also reflects knowledge of our needs. He is the gift who perfectly embodies God's love, generosity and goodness. God's gift came to us in the humblest of wrappings and yet this gift is unparalleled. Paul said:

Thank God for his Son — a gift too wonderful for words!

2 Corinthians 9:15 (NLT)

Jesus told the woman at the well that if she knew the gift of God, she would ask Him for living water. "If you knew the gift of God..." This Gift is very personal – if *you* knew the Gift; your name is on the tag. The amazing thing is that not only are we able to know this Gift, but we are able to share the Gift with others, like the Samaritan. This gift offers unconditional love, unending hope and eternal life to every person who believes in Him. Today you have the opportunity to say thank you to God for His Gift and to invite others to unwrap this Greatest Gift of all.

14

Living the Good Life

For we are His workmanship, created in Christ Jesus for good works, which God prepared beforehand so that we would walk in them.

Ephesians 2:10 (NKJV)

I am one of those people who prefer to prepare ahead of time. If I'm being hospitable and expecting guests, I like to have the casserole ready in the oven and everything set out beforehand. If I'm traveling, the suitcase is packed long before the holiday. In our verse today God is the One who has prepared specific plans for us ahead of time. I love Ephesians 2:10, a power-packed verse. Let's check it out in a few different translations.

For we are God's masterpiece. He has created us anew in Christ Jesus, so we can do the good things He planned for us long ago.

Ephesians 2:10 (NLT)

For we are His creation, created in Christ Jesus for good works, which God prepared ahead of time so that we should walk in them.

Ephesians 2:10 (HCSB)

For we are God's [own] handiwork (His workmanship), recreated in Christ Jesus, [born anew] that we may do those good works which God predestined (planned beforehand) for us [taking paths which He prepared ahead of time], that we should walk in them [living the good life which He prearranged and made ready for us to live].

Ephesians 2:10 (AMP)

- There is a good life that God has already prepared for us.
- There are prepared paths that each one of us ought to walk in.

- There are prearranged good works for us to do along the path of life.

He has a specific path for you today which should make you wake up with excited anticipation and jump out of bed with a spring in your step. He has a path prepared for you that will advance His kingdom, glorify His name, demonstrate His faithfulness and unfailing love, and bring a sense of fulfilment, peace and contentment to your own soul. You are a masterpiece with a Master plan. When God laid out the plan for your life, He lined up the divine connections and the supernatural opportunities and the release of favour to help you fulfil your destiny. Read through the book of Ruth and you will see exactly what I mean. There are bundles of favour on purpose along your pathway. Every morning presents us with another opportunity to fulfil our potential. David testified that…

Your eyes saw my unformed substance, and in Your book all the days [of my life] were written before ever they took shape, when as yet there was none of them.

Psalm 139:16 (AMPC)

You are a loved and cherished one-of-a-kind creation. Each of us has an eternally-designed job description which includes the task, the ability and the place to serve. God knows you better than you know yourself. If you know that you've strayed away from following His purposes, you need to know that it's not too late to begin walking out the paths He has for you. Personalising our verse today makes it even more meaningful to you, especially the last part of the verse which says "…living the good life which He prearranged and made ready for [add your name] to live." We get to walk in prearranged paths – how exciting is that!

15

Keep on Keeping On

Let us not become weary in doing good, for at the proper time we will reap a harvest if we don't give up.

Galatians 6:9 (NIV)

*K*eep on keeping on. This idiom refers to the act of doing what you have been doing but an encouragement to do it more. In other words, persevere. Have endurance. Don't give up. Revelation 2:2 says:

I see what you've done, your hard, hard work, your refusal to quit. I know you can't stomach evil, that you weed out apostolic pretenders. I know your persistence, your courage in my cause that you never wear out.

Revelation 2:2 (MSG)

This is what they were commended for: their refusal to quit and their persistence. Persistence is the key to any worthwhile endeavour. Take the example of prayer. In Luke 18:1 we read:

One day Jesus told his disciples a story to show that they should always pray and never give up.

Luke 18:1 (NLT)

The Amplified Bible puts it:

...they ought always to pray and not to turn coward (faint, lose heart, and give up).

Luke 18:1 (AMP)

To lose heart is to faint, or to turn coward, or to give in. Jesus called for persistence in prayer. Think back to the Old Testament character Elijah. Elijah had to pray seven times for rain. But he persisted. In 1 Kings

18:41 Elijah said, "There is a sound of abundance of rain."[12] As we read on we see Elijah travailing in prayer.

> *Elijah went up to the top of Carmel; and he bowed himself down upon the earth and put his face between his knees. And said to his servant, Go up now, look toward the sea. And he went up and looked and said, There is nothing. Elijah said, Go again seven times. And at the seventh time the servant said, A cloud as small as a man's hand is arising out of the sea. And Elijah said, Go up, say to Ahab, Hitch your chariot and go down, lest the rain stop you. In a little while, the heavens were black with wind-swept clouds, and there was a great rain.*
>
> *1 Kings 18:42-45 (ASV)*

> *He persisted.*

The New Testament mentions Elijah in James 5 and adds the important words which we can easily overlook:

> *Elijah was a man just like us.*
>
> *James 5:17 (ICB)*

In other words, you and I can do it too.

Jesus prayed three times in the Garden of Gethsemane. We are encouraged to keep on asking and keep on seeking in Matthew 7:7-8:

> *"Keep on asking and it will be given you; keep on seeking and you will find; keep on knocking [reverently] and [the door] will be opened to you. For everyone who keeps on asking receives; and he who keeps on seeking finds; and to him who keeps on knocking, [the door] will be opened."*
>
> *Matthew 7:7-8 (AMPC)*

Keep on asking. Keep on seeking. Keep on knocking. Keep on keeping on. Don't get discouraged and give up. Jesus reminded us:

> *...the kingdom of heaven suffereth violence, and the violent take it by force.*
>
> *Matthew 11:12 (KJV)*

Your persistent prayers matter.

---

[12] KJV

December

>...be steadfast, immovable, always abounding in the work of the
Lord, knowing that your labor is not in vain in the Lord.
>
>1 Corinthians 15:58 (ESV)

16

Speak Out for God

I ordained thee a prophet unto the nations. Then said I, Ah, Lord GOD! behold, I cannot speak: for I am a child. But the LORD said unto me, Say not, I am a child: for thou shalt go to all that I shall send thee, and whatsoever I command thee thou shalt speak. Be not afraid of their faces: for I am with thee to deliver thee, saith the LORD. Then the LORD put forth his hand, and touched my mouth. And the LORD said unto me, Behold, I have put my words in thy mouth. See, I have this day set thee over the nations and over the kingdoms, to root out, and to pull down, and to destroy, and to throw down, to build, and to plant.

Jeremiah 1:5-10 (KJV)

I love verse 9: "The LORD put forth his hand and touched my mouth. And the LORD said unto me, Behold, I have put my words in thy mouth." Think of what Jeremiah accomplished after he became God's mouthpiece. He was called to uproot and tear down, to destroy and overthrow, to build and to plant.[13] That's a powerful mission, no small assignment. Through our prayers and witness we can do the same. We need the Lord to touch our mouths and put His words in our mouths so that we pray out God's will. God's Spirit wants to flow through us as rivers of living water.[14] We must believe this, and as the days darken we must learn to be His voice and speak His truth in love. Don't hesitate like Moses. Moses hesitated to accept the mantle of leadership, saying he was slow of speech.[15] But God reminded him:

"Who gave human beings their mouths? ... Is it not I, the LORD? Now go; I will help you speak..."

Exodus 4:11-12 (NIV)

---

[13] See Jeremiah 1:9-10
[14] See John 7:38
[15] See Exodus 4:10

The original language literally says that He would "be with his mouth". God wants to speak through you.

If anyone speaks, they should do so as one who speaks the very words of God.

1 Peter 4:11 (NIV)

Speak as though God Himself were speaking through you. Are you God's mouthpiece in a world that desperately needs to hear His voice? If you examine a musical instrument such as a trombone or clarinet, you will notice that an important aspect of their makeup is the mouthpiece. Yet that mouthpiece is totally useless without a musician. Likewise, we need to allow the Holy Spirit to breathe in us and speak through us.

Peter and John were arrested by the authorities in Jerusalem for speaking out about Jesus. Facing the same religious court that had condemned Jesus to death, Peter (the same Peter who had been so terrified of the opinions of others during the trials of Jesus that he had denied His Lord three times), now filled with the Holy Spirit, boldly proclaimed Jesus Christ as the One...

"...whom you crucified but whom God raised from the dead ... Salvation is found in no one else, for there is no other name under heaven given to men by which we must be saved."

Acts 4:10-12 (NIV)

The authorities were astonished (verse 13). After consultation among themselves they charged John and Peter not to speak at all in the name of Jesus. The disciples' reply was this:

"...we cannot help speaking about what we have seen and heard."

Acts 4:20 (NIV)

It's impossible. If only we had the same courage, the same conviction, the same compulsion to speak out rather than abdicating our responsibility.

17

Walk the Talk

Beloved children, our love can't be an abstract theory we only talk about, but a way of life demonstrated through our loving deeds.

1 John 3:18 (TPT)

ou've just sat down to watch your favourite movie on your tablet. You've really been looking forward to it all day. But instead of being a pleasurable experience, you immediately notice that the picture doesn't quite match the video, making viewing and listening increasingly awkward. You're hearing things that aren't happening in the scene yet. The video might be frozen on a particular point or moving slowly forward while the audio plays happily along. The video may experience lag while the audio continues to play, and the result is confusion.

We are God's audiovisual representatives on earth today. Does your walk match your talk? Does your audio match your video? Do your words and actions match up? You can portray the right outward appearance (your video), but if your words (your audio) do no align with your image then there is something wrong. Being a person of integrity literally means that you are a fully integrated person.

Jesus is the supreme model of integrity. His enemies could only declare:

"Teacher, we know You are truthful and defer to no one, for You don't show partiality but teach truthfully the way of God."

Mark 12:14 (NASB)

The New International Version uses the phrase "man of integrity". Even at the conclusion of His life here on earth as He stood before Pilate, the ruler said:

"I find no grounds for charging this man."

Luke 23:4 (HCSB)

Our profession of faith should be matched by a life of faith.

If we say we have fellowship with him while we walk in darkness, we lie and do not practice the truth. But if we walk in the light, as he is in the light, we have fellowship with one another, and the blood of Jesus his Son cleanses us from all sin.

1 John 1:6-7 (ESV)

If an individual professes to have fellowship with God but the person has a lifestyle of worldliness, that individual lies and does not practise a life of truthfulness.

What are your actions saying? Our words and our deeds should say the same thing. There should be no disparity between them. Paul teaches us:

Look carefully then how you walk, not as unwise but as wise.

Ephesians 5:15 (ESV)

Timothy was told by Paul to set an example "in speech, in conduct, in love, in faith and in purity"[16].

Stop to think about how we are representing God. How often do we really think about how non-believers view us? We should be living out the Good News. We should be walking by faith. We should be demonstrating the love of God. For example, when do you feel the most loved? When someone says "I love you" over and over? Or when someone shows you love by treating you kindly and helping you? The words "I love you" are certainly sweet to hear, but without action they are meaningless. Jesus tells His followers how they will be recognisable: by loving each other.

"By this everyone will know that you are my disciples, if you love one another."

John 13:35 (NIV)

By showing love to others, we exemplify God's love for us. Let's ensure our audio and video are in sync.

---

[16] 1 Timothy 4:12 (NIV)

18

Let Nothing Be Wasted

After everyone was full, Jesus told his disciples, "Now gather the leftovers, so that nothing is wasted." So they picked up the pieces and filled twelve baskets with scraps left by the people who had eaten from the five barley loaves.

John 6:12-13 (NLT)

Another flyer arrived through my letter box. This one is from my local Council advising me to "Be a good elf" this Christmas by reducing my food waste. It states statistics such as:

- £680 is the average cost of food which each UK household throws away each year;
- 74 million mince pies are thrown out;
- and 17,200,000 Brussels sprouts end up in the waste bin.

The flyer is asking everyone to think twice before buying, and reduce food waste this Christmas.

In John's Gospel, we read the story of Jesus feeding the 5,000 hungry people. The people had followed Jesus out of town to listen to His teaching and watch Him heal. They were all still there as mealtime approached. The disciples asked Jesus how He planned to feed the crowd, and Jesus miraculously produced enough food for the crowd from a boy's small lunch of five loaves and two fishes. Once everyone was fed, it seemed the story would end, but Jesus had one more lesson to teach. He instructed the disciples to "gather the leftovers, so that nothing is wasted". For some reason this detail caught my attention. What an extraordinary instruction; what an incredible contrast with the wastefulness of our time. Having miraculously provided this super-abundance of bread, Jesus is deeply concerned that nothing should be wasted. Despite His ability to produce infinite resources, He made this startling statement.

I asked myself what I might be wasting (besides Brussels sprouts!) The answer came swiftly: I unthinkingly waste time and money – at times spending both in ways that benefit no one. I waste opportunities by failing to recognise the *kairos* moment or act upon situations ripe with potential to point those around me to Jesus. I waste my talents and spiritual gifts through neglect and laziness – trading my temporal comfort for eternal impact. Paul instructed:

> *Don't waste your time on useless work, mere busywork, the barren pursuits of darkness.*
>
> Ephesians 5:11 (MSG)

Looking at the life of Jesus, I see intentionality and purpose in His every word, every interaction, every miracle, every healing, every provision. Zero waste; maximum impact. "Let nothing be wasted!"[17] Let these words from the mouth of the Lord Jesus dwell in our hearts to admonish us and to teach us to wisely use what the Lord has put in our hands so that we have zero waste and make maximum impact too.

---

[17] John 6:12 (NIV)

19

Bursting with Health

My son, attend to my words; consent and submit to my sayings. Let them not depart from your sight; keep them in the centre of your heart. For they are life to those who find them, healing and health to all their flesh.

Proverbs 4:20-22 (AMPC)

Fill your thoughts with my words until they penetrate deep into your spirit. Then, as you unwrap my words, they will impart true life and radiant health into the very core of your being.

Proverbs 4:21-22 (TPT)

*I*t's important that as we read the Word, we don't just glance at it and forget it. Don't just read it and walk away; let it change you. We need to spend enough quality time in the Word of God so that we understand it and let it penetrate our hearts. Then it can impart true and radiant health into our beings. Another translation reads:

...listen well to my words;
    tune your ears to my voice.
Keep my message in plain view at all times.
    Concentrate! Learn it by heart!
Those who discover these words live, really live;
    body and soul, they're bursting with health.

Proverbs 4:21-22 (TPT)

God wants us to pay attention to what He is saying because His Word brings life and health. Keep it in plain view at all times. I have Bible verses sellotaped to the inside of my kitchen cupboards and stuck on my fridge with magnets. I have key verses printed in large letters and pinned to my office wall. Why? So that I am constantly reading them and meditating on them, allowing them to sink down into my heart. Reflect on God's words during the day until they "penetrate deep into your spirit".

A few chapters later, we read:

My son, keep my words,
And treasure my commands within you.
Keep my commands and live,
And my law as the apple of your eye.
Bind them on your fingers;
Write them on the tablet of your heart.

Proverbs 7:1-3 (NKJV)

Cherish God's words within your heart.

He sent His word, and healed them,
And delivered them from their destructions.

Psalm 107:20 (NASB)

Prioritise God's Word above all the distractions of life clamouring for your attention. When negative thoughts try to pervade your mind, you need to allow God's truth to renew your thought process to His way of thinking.

Let the word of Christ dwell in you richly...

Colossians 3:16 (ESV)

The Psalmist said:

I have hidden your word in my heart...

Psalm 119:11 (NIV)

The word "hidden" means 'to treasure'. We should handle the Scripture like a priceless gift and make every effort to keep it close to our hearts. When we store it there, we are already furnished with matters of counsel and comfort before the trial comes. The Holy Spirit will bring to remembrance what we need to know at the time we need to know it and we can stand on those verses. When we hide His Word in our hearts we are equipped to minister to others as well. Jesus said:

"...out of the abundance of the heart the mouth speaketh."

Matthew 12:34 (KJV)

When we bank the promises of God's Word in the vault of our hearts, our mouths will have a word in season to share with a weary one. May God's word be in our conversation. May it be in our prayer life. May it give us wisdom in the decisions of life. May it give us encouragement even when circumstances are hard.

20

Supercharged

You've supercharged my life so that I soar again like a flying eagle in the sky.

Psalm 103:5 (TPT)

Your youth, renewed, is like the eagle's [strong, overcoming, soaring]!

Psalm 103:5 (AMP)

*I*n Psalm 103 the Psalmist is considering all the wonderful benefits that come from knowing the Lord and in the process he urges us to "forget not all His benefits"[18]. One of the great benefits mentioned is the forgiveness of all our sins.[19] In the same verse another great benefit is healing:

He heals all your diseases.

Psalm 103:3 (HCSB)

Adding to his list:

[He] redeems your life from the pit and crowns you with love and compassion.

Psalm 103:4 (NIV)

He continues:

[He] satisfies your desires with good things so that your youth is renewed like the eagle's.

Psalm 103:4 (NIV)

Or, as we saw in the Passion Translation, He has "supercharged" our life so that we soar again like a flying eagle. Who doesn't want this?!

---

[18] Psalm 103:2 (NKJV)
[19] See Psalm 103:3

All of these benefits are undeserved and yet God graciously bestows them upon us. What we need is a greater revelation and appreciation of everything that He has done for us.

God renews. God supercharges. He renews our strength. The book of Isaiah says:

> *But those who wait on the LORD shall renew their strength; they shall mount up with wings like eagles, they shall run and not be weary, they shall walk and not faint.*
>
> Isaiah 40:31 (NKJV)

God gives strength to the weary and increases the power of the weak. We are strong in the Lord and in the power of His might. We are designed to be strong, overcoming and soaring. An eagle soars with perfect ease on the wind currents, soaring to heights no other bird can. Runners have a saying for finding the energy they need to finish a race. They call it finding their 'second wind'. There is supposedly a second wind or 'runner's high' that gives you a new burst of energy to finish your race. With the wind of the Spirit, you and I can spread our wings and rise above every problem and soar above the storms of life. He renews us day by day.

> *Therefore we do not become discouraged (utterly spiritless, exhausted, and wearied out through fear). Though our outer man is [progressively] decaying and wasting away, yet our inner self is being [progressively] renewed day after day.*
>
> 2 Corinthians 4:16 (AMP)

We are progressively being renewed day after day as we wait on Him. We are being transformed by the renewing of our minds.[20] We are inwardly renewed with a steadfast spirit, as the Psalmist prayed:

> *Create in me a clean heart, O God, and renew a steadfast spirit within me.*
>
> Psalm 51:10 (ESV)

We are constantly renewed in the spirit of our mind (having a fresh mental and spiritual attitude).[21]

---

[20] See Romans 12:2
[21] See Ephesians 4:23

It's time to stop flapping in our own strength, and soar on the strength and power of the Holy Spirit. Don't be grounded by adversities but let Him supercharge your life. Spread your wings. Day after day let Him sustain you and course your trajectory onward and upward.

21

Sounding the Right Note

*And when they heard that, they lifted up their voice to God with
one accord...*

Acts 4:24 (KJV)

*E*very Christmas I get the opportunity to go and hear the Ballymena
Chamber Orchestra playing their classical pieces by candlelight. It
brings the community together and provides respite from the
hustle and bustle of the season. But imagine a totally different scenario.
The conductor is set to lead the orchestra in Vivaldi's *Winter*. The string
section have tweaked and tuned their instruments. The brass section are
in position. The woodwind are prepared. The percussionists are ready
and waiting. Everyone has a perfect copy of the score to be played. The
guests have taken their seats and the lights are dimming. The conductor
steps forward and with a wave of the hand the signal is given to
commence. However, instead of a beautiful rendition of *Winter*, each
member of the orchestra has decided to play their own personal refrain
and they ignore the conductor. The result is total cacophony, chaos and
confusion. Everyone is disengaged and the air is filled with a disarray of
discordant notes.

Let's move from the concert setting to the prayer room. Is it possible
that the above scene I have described could also apply there? Everyone
has gathered for the purpose of prayer. But instead of praying in unity
and with direction, each prays as he/she likes. The result is a display of
independent thoughts and dissonance. When we pray, the Holy Spirit is
the One who should be the conductor helping us to express a beautiful
rendition of earnest, heart-felt, united, fervent prayer, all for the
advancement of God's kingdom. In the early church we are told that the
believers assembled with united purpose for prayer – no discordant
purposes or selfish agendas.

These all with one mind were continually devoting themselves to prayer [a 'concert of voices' to God], along with the women, and Mary the mother of Jesus, and with His brothers.

Acts 1:14 (NASB)

And when the day of Pentecost was fully come, they were all with one accord in one place.

Acts 2:1 (KJV)

And day after day they regularly assembled in the temple with united purpose...

Acts 2:46 (AMPC)

In Acts 4:24 we see this united purpose again.

And when they heard that, they lifted up their voice to God with one accord.

Acts 4:24 (KJV)

The Greek word for "one accord" is *homothumadon.* It literally refers to a concert of voices that are in a state of union, with one mind and one passion. It's a musical term that means to strike the same notes together. It produces a harmonious prayer of beautifully coordinated hearts and minds.

We have a common score in God's Word. When we, as God's instruments of righteousness, submit to the Holy Spirit as our prayer conductor and use the sheet music of Scripture to guide us, there is harmony and cohesion. We are told to pray in the Spirit. We should be "praying at all times in the Spirit, with all prayer and supplication"[22]. This type of prayer shook prison doors open in the book of Acts. It brought about exponential growth as many were added to their number. When we pray in accordance with God's Spirit, we can pray according to God's will and be confident of His perfect answer to our requests. May we sound the same note and see God's will be done on earth as it is in heaven.

---

[22] Ephesians 6:18 (ESVUK)

22

Him Possible

For nothing will be impossible with God.

Luke 1:37 (NASB)

*W*hen the angel Gabriel appeared to Mary and told her that she would give birth to Israel's promised Messiah, she was stunned. *How can this be?*

And the angel answered and said to her, "The Holy Spirit will come upon you, and the power of the Highest will overshadow you; therefore, also, that Holy One who is to be born will be called the Son of God. Now indeed, Elizabeth your relative has also conceived a son in her old age; and this is now the sixth month for her who was called barren. For with God nothing will be impossible."

Luke 1:35-37 (NASB)

The angel told Mary, "For with God nothing will be impossible." The literal Greek text says, "For no word from God is void of power." The Amplified Bible translates it:

"For with God nothing is ever impossible and no word from God shall be without power or impossible of fulfilment."

Luke 1:35-37 (AMP)

In Jeremiah, God asked:

"Behold, I am the LORD, the God of all flesh. Is there anything too hard for Me?"

Jeremiah 32:27 (NKJV)

Jeremiah stated in the same chapter:

"O Sovereign LORD! You made the heavens and earth by your strong hand and powerful arm. Nothing is too hard for you!"

Jeremiah 32:27 (NLT)

It's impossible – but it is *Him*-possible! God says to us:

"When you're in over your head, I'll be there with you.
*   When you're in rough waters, you will not go down.*
When you're between a rock and a hard place,
*   it won't be a dead end –*
Because I am GOD, your personal God,
*   The Holy of Israel, your Savior."*

Isaiah 43:2-3 (MSG)

In over their head; in rough waters; between a rock and a hard place. Sound familiar? Recall what God said about each of these:

In over your head? I will be there for you.

In rough waters? You will not go down.

Between a rock and a hard place? It won't be a dead end.

Why? Because I am God, your personal God.

You may be looking at your circumstances and saying to yourself, it's impossible. If so, remember it is Him-possible! That was Paul's attitude:

I can do all things through Him who strengthens me.

Philippians 4:13 (NASB)

Paul did not say "I can't" – that is the language of pessimism. Paul did not say "I can" – that is the language of presumption. He said "I can ... through Christ" – that is the language of power. Remember that with God nothing is ever impossible and no word from God shall be without power or impossible of fulfilment.

23

Cinnamon, the Finest Spice

*Now it is God who makes both us and you stand firm in Christ.
He anointed us, set his seal of ownership on us, and put his Spirit
in our hearts as a deposit, guaranteeing what is to come.*

2 Corinthians 1:21-22 (NIVUK)

*T*here are certain smells in life that remind us of specific times, seasons and family. One such is the comforting aroma of cinnamon. It is synonymous with Christmas, candles, cakes, *pot pourri* (cinnamon sticks) and hot drinks. Cinnamon has been used for centuries. The Lord said to Moses:

Take the finest spices: of liquid myrrh 500 shekels, and of sweet-smelling cinnamon half as much, that is, 250, and 250 of aromatic cane, and 500 of cassia, according to the shekel of the sanctuary, and a hin of olive oil. And you shall make of these a sacred anointing oil blended as by the perfumer; it shall be a holy anointing oil.

Exodus 30:23-25 (ESV)

This highly perfumed oil was used to consecrate (set apart) the articles used in Temple worship, including the ark of the testimony, the holy tabernacle, and all its furnishings, which made them "holy" unto the Lord.

The anointing oil included cinnamon as one of its five ingredients. To be "anointed" is to be made sacred (consecrated); to be set apart and dedicated to serve God; to be endowed with enabling gifts and grace; to be divinely designated, inaugurated or chosen for a special purpose. The Greek word for 'anoint' is *chrio* from which the title 'Christ' derives. Christ means 'the Anointed One'. Therefore Christmas means 'celebration (mass) of the Anointed One'. Martha said to Jesus:

"I believe thou art the Christ, the Son of God."

John 11:27 (KJV)

On another occasion Peter declared:

"You are the Christ, the Son of the living God."

Matthew 16:16 (ESV)

At Jesus' interrogation by the Jews before His crucifixion, the high priest demanded:

"...tell us if You are the Christ, the Son of God."

Matthew 26:63 (ESV)

At the beginning of His ministry on earth, Jesus went to the synagogue in Nazareth on the Sabbath and read the Scripture for the day. Luke says:

And when He had opened the book, He found the place where it was written:
"The Spirit of the Lord is upon Me,
Because He has anointed Me
To preach the gospel to the poor;
He has sent Me to heal the brokenhearted,
To proclaim liberty to the captives
And recovery of sight to the blind,
To set at liberty those who are oppressed;
To proclaim the acceptable year of the Lord."
Then He closed the book, and gave it back to the attendant and sat down. And the eyes of all who were in the synagogue were fixed on Him. And He began to say to them, "Today this Scripture is fulfilled in your hearing."

Luke 4:17-21 (NKJV)

He is the Anointed One but the Bible tells us further:

He anointed us, set his seal of ownership on us, and put his Spirit in our hearts as a deposit, guaranteeing what is to come.

2 Corinthians 1:21-22 (NIVUK)

John said that Christians...

...have an anointing from the Holy One, and all of you know the truth.

1 John 2:20 (NIVUK)

It's the divine enablement to fulfil a divine purpose. All believers are anointed by God. The question is not, "Are we anointed?" but, "Will we use the anointing the Lord has given us to fully live out our faith and give the highest honour and glory to God?"

24

Behold

And the angel said unto them, Fear not: for, behold, I bring you good tidings of great joy, which shall be to all people. For unto you is born this day in the city of David a Saviour, which is Christ the Lord.

Luke 2:10-11 (KJV)

The word "behold" is so powerful. It is a pity that some of our more modern translations have done away with "behold" because it is seen as an archaic word. "Behold!" the angel said. The word means 'to see'. However, in the Bible it is generally used to mean more than merely seeing with the natural eye. What the angel was telling Mary to behold had not yet happened and could not yet be seen in the natural. The angel was drawing Mary's attention to the spiritual. This is not less real than the natural, but *more* real, because the natural comes forth from the spiritual by the Word of God. It takes spiritual vision to see the great things God desires to bring forth in the natural. So, 'beholding' is allowing the eyes of our heart[23] to be enlightened and focused on Jesus.

Consider the impact of "behold" in the following verses:

Therefore the Lord himself shall give you a sign; Behold a virgin shall conceive, and bear a son, and shall call his name Immanuel.

Isaiah 7:14 (KJV)

"Behold! The Lamb of God who takes away the sin of the world!"

John 1:29 (NKJV)

Behold what manner of love the Father has bestowed on us, that we should be called children of God!

1 John 3:1 (NKJV)

---

[23] See Ephesians 1:18

"Behold, I give you the authority to trample on serpents and scorpions, and over all the power of the enemy, and nothing shall by any means hurt you."

Luke 10:19 (NKJV)

"Behold, I stand at the door, and knock: if any man hear my voice, and open the door, I will come in to him, and will sup with him, and he with me."

Revelation 3:20 (KJV)

God tells Ezekiel that his people...

...have eyes to see but do not see, and ears to hear but do not hear...

Ezekiel 12:2 (AMP)

May that not describe us. In the words of Paul:

And [I pray] that the eyes of your heart [the very centre and core of your being] may be enlightened [flooded with light by the Holy Spirit], so that you will know and cherish the hope [the divine guarantee, the confident expectation] to which He has called you, the riches of His glorious inheritance in the saints (God's people).

Ephesians 1:18 (AMP)

It's time to behold.

25

Gloria in Excelsis Deo

...the glory of the Lord shone around them...

Luke 2:9 (ESV)

*I*t's beginning to look a lot like Christmas, or at least smell like it and sound like it. The air is filled with the aroma of gingerbread cookies, minty candy canes, fresh pine, mince pies and cinnamon candles. Traditional carols, festive films, Christmas cards all make their annual appearance. One word which is repeated time and again in our Christmas songs and readings is the word "glory".

Isaiah had prophesied many years ago:

...the glory of the LORD shall be revealed...

Isaiah 40:5 (ESV)

The whole concept of the glory of the Lord surrounds the Christmas scene. On the night Jesus was born something spectacular took place. The plains of Bethlehem became the theatre for one of the most spectacular sound-and-light shows in human history.

And there were shepherds living out in the fields nearby, keeping watch over their flocks at night. An angel of the Lord appeared to them, and the glory of the Lord shone around them, and they were terrified.

Luke 2:8-9 (NIVUK)

The glory of the Lord shone around them. Can you imagine what this must have been like? This is an astounding statement. Verse 13 continues the story:

Suddenly a great company of the heavenly host appeared with the angel, praising God and saying, "Glory to God in the highest heaven..."

Luke 2:13 (NIVUK)

This is where we derive the chorus from *Angels We Have Heard On High*, "Gloria in Excelsius Deo." (Latin for "Glory to God in the highest.") We can't help but sing about the glory of Christmas. But I wonder if we understand the depth of the word?

In John the birth of Jesus is described in this way:

The Word was made flesh, and dwelt among us, and we beheld His glory, the glory as of the only begotten of the Father, full of grace and truth.

John 1:14 (NKJV)

We beheld His glory. This glory is "beheld". The original viewers of the first Christmas perceived Christ's glory.

The Son is the radiance of God's glory.

Hebrews 1:3

May the glory of the Lord surround us and shine into our communities. May we be able to say this Christmas, "We beheld His glory." Having looked beyond the tinsel to the Truth of His Word, may we perceive afresh "the Lord of glory"[24]. May we "contemplate the Lord's glory" and be "transformed into His image with ever-increasing glory"[25]. May our lives billboard to the world, "Glory to God in the highest." Now there's coming a day, according to the prophet Habakkuk, when the earth will be "filled with the knowledge of the glory of the Lord, as the waters cover the sea"[26].

---

[24] 1 Corinthians 2:8 (AMP)
[25] 2 Corinthians 3:18 (NIVUK)
[26] Habakkuk 2:14 (KJV)

26

Cardboard Boxes

Whoever is generous to the poor lends to the LORD,
  and he will repay him for his deed.

Proverbs 19:17 (ESV)

Someone once quipped, "The best gift doesn't come in a box; it *is* the box." After tracking down the perfect toy for Christmas, many parents see their child abandon it to play with the box instead. Cardboard boxes can engage children for hours and inspire creativity and imagination as the children build upon, transform and reinvent them. With nothing more than a little creativity, boxes can be transformed into forts or houses, spaceships or submarines, castles or caves, rowboats, robots, time machines, puppet stages etc. This is a great way to develop your child's spatial awareness and encourage exploration.

Boxing Day is the name we give to the 26th of December. While government buildings and small businesses are closed, the shopping malls are filled with people either exchanging gifts or buying reduced-price Christmas gifts, cards and decorations. Many children like to go and spend their gift vouchers that they received on Christmas Day. But why is it called Boxing Day? It is generally accepted that the name derives from the giving of Christmas 'boxes'. December 26 was the day centuries ago when lords of the manor and aristocrats typically distributed Christmas boxes, often filled with small gifts, money and leftovers from Christmas dinner, to their household servants and employees, who were required to work on December 25, in recognition of good service throughout the year. These boxes were, in essence, holiday bonuses. According to some sources, Boxing Day can also be traced back to the Victorian era when churches often displayed a box into which their parishioners put donations. Alms boxes were placed in churches during the Advent season for the collection of monetary donations. Clergy members distributed the contents of the boxes to the poor on December 26, which is also the feast of St. Stephen, the first Christian martyr and a figure known for acts of charity. Ireland celebrates December 26 as St. Stephen's Day. All this reminds us of today's verse.

The consequence for ignoring the plight of the poor is also made clear in another proverb:

Whoever oppresses a poor man insults his Maker,
but he who is generous to the needy honours him.

Proverbs 14:31 (ESV)

God's people cannot be indifferent toward those in need, because His expectations for us in regard to taking care of His poor are woven throughout the entirety of Scripture. In the New Testament Jesus said to His disciples, "*when* you give..." not, "*if* you give..."[27] John instructs:

If anyone has material possessions and sees his brother in need but has no pity on him, how can the love of God be in him? Dear children, let us not love with words or tongue but with action and in truth.

1 John 3:17-18 (NIVUK)

May we celebrate the true essence of Boxing Day and share generously with those in need.

---

[27] Matthew 6:2 (NIVUK)

27

Come

And they came with haste and found Mary and Joseph, and the Babe lying in a manger.

Luke 2:16 (NKJV)

*T*he *Telegraph* newspaper had a vote for the most popular and well-liked carol and this was the result of the top four. *Hark, the Herald Angels Sing* (18%); *Silent Night* (16%); *In the Bleak Midwinter* (12%); *O Come, all ye Faithful* (11%).

O Come, all ye Faithful is a beautiful carol inviting us all to come and behold our Lord. Think of the lyrics:

O come, all ye faithful
Joyful and triumphant,
O come ye, O come ye to Bethlehem.
Come and behold Him,
Born the King of Angels;
O come, let us adore Him,
O come, let us adore Him,
O come, let us adore Him,
Christ the Lord.

'Come' is a word often on the lips of Jesus. Let's remind ourselves of some examples:

"Come to me, all who labor and are heavy laden, and I will give you rest. Take my yoke upon you, and learn from me, for I am gentle and lowly in heart, and you will find rest for your souls. For my yoke is easy, and my burden is light."

Matthew 11:28-30 (ESV)

"If anyone thirsts, let him come to Me and drink. He who believes in Me, as the Scripture has said, out of his heart will flow rivers of living water."

John 7:37-39 (NKJV)

And He said to them, Come after Me [as disciples – letting Me be your Guide], follow Me, and I will make you fishers of men!

Matthew 4:19 (AMPC)

"Come away by yourselves to a secluded place and rest a little while."

Mark 6:31 (AMP)

"Come and have breakfast."

John 21:12 (AMP)

One day may we hear our King say:

"Come, you who are blessed of My Father, inherit the kingdom prepared for you from the foundation of the world. For I was hungry, and you gave Me something to eat; I was thirsty, and you gave Me something to drink; I was a stranger, and you invited Me in; naked, and you clothed Me; I was sick, and you visited Me; I was in prison, and you came to Me."

Matthew 25:34-36 (ESV)

Relish each of these wonderful invitations and come to Him and experience rest, rivers of living water, and reach out to others with the same life-changing message.

28

Let Your Light Shine

The people who walked in darkness
Have seen a great light;
Those who dwelt in the land of the shadow of death,
Upon them a light has shined.

Isaiah 9:2 (NKJV)

*L*ights are a symbol of hope, warmth and excitement. No wonder I embrace the ambiance of Christmas with the strings of Christmas streetlights; beautiful lanterns, candlelight, even the spectacular northern lights are visible from time to time. Isn't it amazing that God is called the "Father of lights"[28]? Jesus is the "light of the world"[29]! We are called "into his wonderful light"[30]!

A painter painted a bleak picture of a winter scene. It depicted a storm sweeping across the countryside. Over in the corner there was a cabin, but it still looked dead and hopeless. But with one small stroke, the painter dramatically transformed the picture. He took the tip of his brush, dipped it in gold paint, touched one window of the cabin, and the golden glow from that cabin transformed the picture from coldness to invitation to come in; from a picture of death to life, from a picture of gloom to gladness. Jesus said:

"I have come as Light into the world, so that everyone who believes in Me will not remain in darkness."

John 12:46 (NASB)

We love to sing, "Silent night, holy night," but this great carol is not about night or darkness. It's about the light.

B

---

[28] James 1:17 (NKJV)
[29] John 8:12 (NKJV)
[30] 1 Peter 2:9 (NIV)

Son of God,
Love's pure light
Radiant beams from Thy holy face,
With the dawn of redeeming grace.

When we sing *Hark, the Herald Angels Sing*, we say:

Hail the Son of righteousness!
Light and life to all He brings,
Risen with healing in His wings.

Isaiah reminds us of the birth of Christ:

The people who walked in darkness have seen a great light: those who lived in a land of deep darkness – on them light has shined ... for a child has been born for us, a son given to us.

Isaiah 9:2,6 (ESVUK)

Jesus tells us:

"You are the light of the world. A city set on a hill cannot be hidden; nor does anyone light a lamp and put it under a basket, but on the lampstand, and it gives light to all who are in the house. Let your light shine before men in such a way that they may see your good works, and glorify your Father who is in heaven."

Matthew 5:14 (NASB)

Paul picks up on this as well when he says:

For at one time you were darkness, but now you are light in the Lord. Walk as children of the light...

Ephesians 5:8 (NKJV)

It's a simple message: *let your light shine.* Don't hide your testimony. Relay hope and realise the strength of collective light. Each house in a city with its light on casts a glow across the sky. The combined impact of many lights together illustrates the effect of a community of disciples on the surrounding darkness. In the words of Isaiah 60:1:

Arise, shine;
For your light has come!

Isaiah 60:1 (NKJV)

29

If I Were a Shepherd

There were shepherds out in the field, keeping watch over their flock by night. And an angel of the Lord appeared to them, and the glory of the Lord shone around them.

Luke 2:8-9 (ESV)

*I*n the Christmas carol *In the Bleak Midwinter*, verse 4 says, "If I were a shepherd, I would bring a lamb." When it comes to casting a Christmas nativity play, shepherds rank low on the list of desirable parts. The most coveted roles, of course, go to Mary and Joseph. After that, I expect that the three wise men get top billing. Being one of the magi is special too because you get to dress as royalty and bear precious gifts. Being an angel gives you a shining role and you get to broadcast a life-changing message. As for being one of the shepherds, however, you get to wear a dressing gown and tie a tea towel on your head!

Imagine being one of those shepherds in Bethlehem, watching your sheep at night. Try to imagine this incredible event unfolding before you as an angel of the Lord comes to deliver a message. Luke says:

And in the same region there were shepherds out in the field, keeping watch over their flock by night. And an angel of the Lord appeared to them, and the glory of the Lord shone around them, and they were filled with fear. And the angel said to them, "Fear not, for behold, I bring you good news of great joy that will be for all the people. For unto you is born this day in the city of David a Saviour, who is Christ the Lord."

Luke 2:8-11

After the 400 'silent years', God now speaks through angels to lowly shepherds on a remote hillside outside an obscure Judean village. To fully fit the profile of a shepherd, you would have to fall into the category of insignificant, marginal, disregarded by society and religious outcasts. In those days being a shepherd was a lowly job. Shepherds were not even allowed to be witnesses in a court of law. Yet God chose those lowly shepherds for a special duty. God chose shepherds to be the messengers of Jesus' birth. Their part in the Christmas story helps us to see that everyone is important to God. You may think of yourself as someone who is on the 'outside' of things – looking in. You may even feel 'out in the cold' so to speak. But this message is for you. His love is all-inclusive.

Notice, while the shepherds first reacted in fear, they soon responded in faith. They acted on what they heard. They turned to one another and basically said, "Let's go and see this for ourselves – and let's go now!" They realised that the news they had heard wasn't a 'page five' story, but a front page headline that would change the world forever. They chose to believe. Note the exact wording. They didn't say, "Let's go and see if these things are true." They said, "Let's go and see this thing that has come to pass." It's not enough to hear about Jesus. It's not enough to glimpse the manger and think that this is a great nostalgic narrative and go on your merry way. It's about your response to the angel's life-changing message. It's about believing and acting on what you have heard. God transformed an ordinary evening into an extraordinary experience that had effects for all eternity. The shepherds returned to their jobs "glorifying and praising God for all the things they had heard and seen"[31]. The celebration of Christmas is a special season, but when the merriment and excitement is over, will we return to our jobs and our responsibilities glorifying and praising God?

---

[31] Luke 2:20 (NIV)

30

We Have Come to Worship Him

Where is He that is born King of the Jews? for we have seen his star in the east, and are come to worship Him.

Matthew 2:2 (KJV)

The wise men (or magi) had come to Jerusalem with a burning question: "Where is He that is born King of the Jews?" In Greek the emphasis is on the word *born*. It's a contrast to Herod, who grasped his position through political manipulation. Jesus, on the other hand, was "born" king of the Jews. They said, "We've come to bow before Him in worship."[32] Indeed, as we read on through Matthew 2 we discover that they were provided with the opportunity to worship.

And when they were come into the house, they saw the young child with Mary his mother, and fell down, and worshipped him: and when they had opened their treasures, they presented unto him gifts; gold, and frankincense and myrrh.

Matthew 2:11

What is the meaning of the word "worship"? How can their experience enhance your worship? In the original Greek it is *proskuneo* – a word which comes from the Greek words *pros* ('to' or 'toward') and *kuneo* ('to kiss'). It literally means 'to kiss the hand (toward) someone in token of reverence'. It means 'to prostrate oneself, to lay on the floor in homage'. Among the Orientals, especially the Persians, it portrays a subject bowing in honour at the feet of their king – an expression of profound reverence and submission. Our word 'worship' comes from the Old English 'weorthscipe', which means worthiness. We *worship* someone because they are *worth* the respect they receive. Worship is the only fitting response to the King of kings.

---

[32] TPT

For the magi, worship was their sole intention, the purpose of their journey. Distance wasn't a barrier to them. They came expecting to encounter. They came prepared for worship. They were overjoyed at the prospect of it. When the magi saw that the star had come to a stop right over the house where the child was, they were overjoyed. In the original Greek, four different words are used to express their joy, which cannot be adequately expressed in English. As the Revised Standard Version translates verse 10:

> *When they saw the star, they rejoiced exceedingly with great joy...*
>
> *Matthew 2:10 (RSV)*

A modern paraphrase put it this way:

> *...they were so ecstatic that they shouted and celebrated with unrestrained joy.*
>
> *Matthew 2:10 (TPT)*

Is this a description of our worship? We join with heaven in singing His praise. Today He is seated in the place of honour. Revelation says:

> *The four and twenty elders fall down before him that sat on the throne, and worship him that liveth for ever and ever, and cast their crowns before the throne, saying, Thou art worthy, O Lord, to receive glory and honour and power: for thou hast created all things, and for thy pleasure they are and were created.*
>
> *Revelation 4:10 (KJV*

Come, let us worship Him.

31

Good News

And the angel said to them, "Do not be afraid; for behold, I bring you good news of great joy which shall be for all the people."

Luke 2:10 (AMP)

... "Don't be afraid. For I have come to bring you good news, the most joyous news the world has ever heard! And it is for everyone everywhere!"

Luke 2:10 (TPT)

The word 'gospel' literally means 'good news'. It is indeed the most joyous news the world has ever heard and it's for everyone everywhere! "Gospel" is the translation of the Greek noun *euangelion,* meaning 'good news', and the verb *euangelizo,* meaning 'to bring or announce good news'. Both words are derived from the Greek word *eu* which means 'good' and the noun *angelos,* 'messenger'. In classical Greek, a *euangelos* was one who brought a message of victory or other political or personal news that caused joy. Paul stated:

Now, brothers and sisters, I want to remind you of the gospel I preached to you, which you received and on which you have taken your stand. By this gospel you are saved, if you hold firmly to the word I preached to you. Otherwise, you have believed in vain. For what I received I passed on to you as of first importance: that Christ died for our sins according to the Scriptures, that he was buried, that he was raised on the third day according to the Scriptures.

1 Corinthians 15:1-4 (NIV)

How we need good news. It is news when it is shared ("the gospel I preached to you"). It is good when it is received and applied to people's lives ("which you received and on which you have taken your stand").

Are we doing our part to share the good news with others? Everyone loves to hear good news, and that has been true for centuries. Almost 3,000 years ago Solomon penned the following proverb:

A cheerful look brings joy to the heart;
  good news makes for good health.

Proverbs 15:30 (NLT)

Take the opportunity of the spirit of the Christmas season to spread the wonderful news of Christ. Tell others the good news: that God sent His only Son to earth to pay the price of our sin. Point others to the true meaning of this season. What better news is there to take than the message that God has made a way for us to be reconciled to Him? Paul's single-minded focus to fulfil his responsibility of sharing the gospel as widely as possible should energise us all. He said:

But none of these things move me, neither count I my life dear unto myself, so that I might finish my course with joy, and the ministry, which I have received of the Lord Jesus, to testify the gospel of the grace of God.

Acts 20:24 (KJV)

Have we received and applied the good news to our lives? Are we taking our stand on its truth? Are we conducting ourselves in a manner worthy of the gospel of Christ? Remind yourself about what God has done for you in Christ and who you are in Him. Don't settle for a purely cerebral form of the gospel which is exclusively head knowledge; it must be experiential and impact the heart and transform us from the inside out. In cloaked compliance from childhood we may have memorised many gospel verses, but that knowledge must be applied to our lives. Then it is truly "good".

January

January

1

Do It All

And whatever you do, whether in word or deed, do it all in the name of the Lord Jesus, giving thanks to God the Father through Him.

Colossians 3:17 (NIVUK)

At the threshold of a brand-new year let us emphatically embrace the magnitude of the "all"-encompassing statements in the Bible. Believe for the manifestation of "all" in your life this year. Do not settle for *some* when God says *all*. For example:

Surely your goodness and love will follow me all the days of my life...

Psalm 23:6 (NIVUK)

That means, *every* day of this year and beyond, with no exceptions. There will never be a day in which the abundant goodness and mercy of the Lord are not present and in pursuit.

Cast all your anxiety on him because he cares for you...

1 Peter 5:7 (NIV)

...and give Him your burdens and worries. Now is the time to jettison the load for the amazing journey ahead. Remember:

God is able to bless you abundantly, so that in all things at all times, having all that you need, you will abound in every good work...

2 Corinthians 9:8 (NIVUK)

Marinate in those words: in *all* things, at *all* times, having *all* you need. Jesus said:

...all things are possible to him who believes.

Mark 9:23 (NKJV)

Nothing is too hard for God. He did not say *some* things are possible, but *all* things are possible to him who believes. The only limitation is in our believing. Take the limits off and see the awesomeness of our God; dream big dreams as you take your stand on His exceeding great and precious promises which are all "yes" and "Amen" in Christ[33]. The invitation awaits your acceptance to...

> *Trust in the Lord with all your heart*
> > *and do not lean on your own understanding.*
> *In all your ways acknowledge him,*
> > *and he will make your paths straight.*
>
> *Proverbs 3:5-6 (ESV)*

Don't forget to be thankful for all God's benefits given to us as His children.

> *Bless the Lord, O my soul: and all that is within me, bless his holy name.*
> *Bless the Lord, O my soul, and forget not all his benefits:*
> *Who forgiveth all thine iniquities; who healeth all thy diseases.*
>
> *Psalm 103:1-3 (KJV)*

Establish His benefits deep within your heart and live in the fullness of what God has provided for you. Remember that prayer is the great essential and we should be...

> *...praying always with all prayer and supplication in the Spirit, and watching thereunto with all perseverance and supplication for all saints.*
>
> *Ephesians 6:18 (KJV)*

Just as breathing is crucial to our physical well-being, so is prayer to our spiritual well-being. Finally:

> *And whatever you do, whether in word or deed, do it all in the name of the Lord Jesus, giving thanks to God the Father through him.*
>
> *Colossians 3:17 (NIVUK)*

Paul said in another letter to another church:

---

[33] 2 Corinthians 1:20 (NASB)

...whatever you do, do all to the glory of God.

1 Corinthians 10:31 (NKJV)

May God get all the glory in our lives today and always.

2

The Brook Dried Up

It happened after a while that the brook dried up, because there was no rain in the land.

1 Kings 17:7 (NASB)

I have been contemplating the ramifications of 1 Kings 17:7 and specifically the words "the brook dried up". Elijah was well supplied, morning and evening, by the miraculous special delivery meals of the ravens. In addition, God provided plenty of refreshing water from the splashing brook that flowed nearby. The brook represented a place of provision and plenty.

However, we go on to read the words, "...the brook dried up."

Elijah had the choice of bemoaning the fact that the brook no longer flowed or choosing to move on with God's plan. God's provision for Elijah, and his assignment, was in another location. God told him:

"Arise, go to Zarephath, which belongs to Sidon, and stay there; behold, I have commanded a widow there to provide for you."

1 Kings 17:9

Had the brook not dried up, Elijah would have stayed there. He would have relaxed in his comfort zone. But he would have missed out on the miraculous widow's cruse of oil and barrel of meal, the raising of the widow's son, the Carmel experience and fire from heaven, being fed by an angel, dividing the waters of the Jordan, mentoring Elisha and so much more.

When the waters of the brook stop flowing and the ravens stop flying with food in their mouths, let us take note that the season has changed and it's time to move on to the next great part of God's plan. In the brook, note that God only fed one person, Elijah; but when it dried up, God sent Elijah to a family and God used him to feed a bigger number, and when Elijah left this family, he was used by God to release rain and a whole nation was fed and refreshed.

When one assignment ends, don't sit by the brook complaining. Move on because God has something bigger and greater in store.

3

Uncharted Waters

"...you have not passed this way before."

Joshua 3:4 (NASB)

*T*he people of Israel had finally ended their wilderness wanderings. Joshua and his people were looking forward to entering Canaan, the promised land, and taking possession of it, and now the time had come.

> *"When you see the Ark of the Covenant of the LORD your God with the Levitical priests carrying it, then you shall set out from your place and go after it. However, there shall be between you and it a distance of about 2,000 cubits by measure. Do not come near it, that you may know the way by which you shall go, for you have not passed this way before." Then Joshua said to the people, "Consecrate yourselves, for tomorrow the LORD will do wonders among you."*

Joshua 3:3-5 (NASB)

Notice the words "for you have not passed this way before".

In other words, you're about to go down a road which is new to you. It's a new chapter, a new adventure with God. You're about to travel through unknown territory, untrodden ways, uncharted waters. That, in principle, is exactly where you and I stand right now as we embark upon a brand-new year.

What guidelines does this passage offer us this year? Let's consider some of them over the next four days. Today's advice is this: *let God lead you.*

In verse 3, the officers told the Israelites to "go after" the Ark. Why? "...that you may know the way by which you shall go..." The Ark of the Covenant is mentioned eight times in Joshua 3.[34] To the Israelites, the

---

[34] Verses 3,6,8,11,13,14,15,17

Ark symbolised the Presence of God. They were to pursue the Presence of God. In other words, when God moved, they were to move. When God stopped, they were to do the same.

As the people prepared to go into new territory, they were to follow their God who went before them. In a similar manner we need to prioritise the Presence of God in our lives. Pursue Him. Follow His lead. Don't rush ahead and don't lag behind. God required the Israelites to stay 2,000 cubits (1,000 yards) behind the Ark. This was for two reasons. Firstly, to respect the holy nature of the Ark of the Covenant. Secondly, it was to make sure that everyone had a clear view of it. Israel would accomplish this impossible task as they set their eyes upon God's Presence, and followed only after His Presence.

4

Consecrate Yourselves

Then Joshua said to the people, "Consecrate yourselves, for tomorrow the LORD will do wonders among you."

Joshua 3:5 (NASB)

The second guideline for making it victoriously through unknown territory is this: *consecrate yourselves.* In other words, God was telling His people that if they were going to cross what seemed to be an impassable river and follow His will, they must be set apart for Him. The word "consecrate" is the Hebrew word *kawdash* – it means 'to be holy, sanctified, set apart'. The related word *kadosh* is the word uttered by the angels who minister around the throne of God crying out day and night: *kadosh, kadosh, kadosh;* holy, holy, holy.

Consecration is a call to address anything that would contaminate your relationship with God. It is a call to holiness and obedience in every particular area of our lives. Nothing less will do. Do we need a renewed sense that we are a people holy unto the Lord? Absolutely. Paul tells us:

Therefore, I urge you, brothers and sisters, in view of God's mercy, to offer your bodies as a living sacrifice, holy and pleasing to God – this is your true and proper worship. Do not conform to the pattern of this world, but be transformed by the renewing of your mind. Then you will be able to test and approve what God's will is – his good, pleasing and perfect will.

Romans 12:1-2 (NIV)

We are to be set apart from sin and set apart for service unto God. We are to be clean vessels for Him to use.

He will be a vessel for honor, sanctified, useful to the Master, prepared for every good work.

2 Timothy 2:21 (NASB)

May God himself, the God of peace, sanctify you through and through. May your whole spirit, soul and body be kept blameless at the coming of our Lord Jesus Christ. The one who calls you is faithful and He will do it.

1 Thessalonians 5:23-24 (NIVUK)

"...sanctify you through and through" – wholly, solely for His glory. It was in Dublin in 1873 that D. L. Moody heard British evangelist Henry Varley utter those life-changing words:

The world has yet to see what God can do with and for and through and in a man who is fully and wholly consecrated to Him.

Prepare yourself for tomorrow by consecrating yourself today.

5

Get Your Feet Wet

When the feet of the priests who carry the ark of the LORD, the Lord of all the earth, come to rest in the Jordan's waters, its waters will be cut off. The water flowing downstream will stand up [in] a mass.

Joshua 3:13 (HCSB)

*H*ere we have the third guideline for getting through unfamiliar territory victoriously: *get your feet wet*. The command of God to step into the water called for them to get their feet wet. The events described here took place during the flood season, when the Jordan River was much deeper than usual and extremely wide – probably a mile wide at some points. During the flood season, the current was swift. It was spring (March-April), towards the end of the rainy season.[35] Coupled with the melting snows of Mount Hermon, the Jordan River became a formidable obstacle. The Jordan was defiantly uncrossable! But God can turn a 'no way' into a highway. The great question that loomed over the camp of Israel and over our lives today is, *will we walk by sight or by faith? Do we really believe God can handle the impossible?*

So when the people set out from their tents to cross the Jordan with the priests carrying the ark of the covenant before the people, and when those who carried the ark came into the Jordan, and the feet of the priests carrying the ark were dipped in the edge of the water (for the Jordan overflows all its banks all the days of harvest), the waters which were flowing down from above stood and rose up in one heap, a great distance away at Adam, the city that is beside Zarethan; and those which were flowing down toward the sea of the Arabah, the Salt Sea, were completely cut off. So the people crossed opposite Jericho. And the priests who carried the ark of the covenant of the LORD stood firm on dry

---

[35] See Joshua 4:19

ground in the middle of the Jordan while all Israel crossed on dry ground, until all the nation had finished crossing the Jordan.

Joshua 3:14-17 (NASB)

There is a time to step into the water. If you want God to guide you through the unexplored territory of this year, and take you through your Jordans of difficulty, you are going to have to 'get your feet wet'. That is, you are going to have to put your faith in action. You must be willing to step out by faith and trust God to do the rest.

6

Expect a Miracle

Then Joshua said to the people, "Consecrate yourselves, for tomorrow the LORD will do wonders among you."

Joshua 3:5 (NASB)

*I*n Joshua 3, as this community prepares to move and claim new territory, God reminds the people to expect amazing things. The people of Israel were to expect God to work a miracle. God is still in the business of performing miracles. God wants to do wondrous things in all of our lives. Are you prepared for that? Where is your state of expectancy? Whatever it is that holds us hostage in life, we need to focus on the God of miracles, not on the size of the problem. Psalm 42:11 encouragingly advises:

Oh, my soul, don't be discouraged. Don't be upset. Expect God to act!

Psalm 42:11 (TLB).

We need to be reminded that God has said He will do exceedingly and abundantly above all we can think or imagine. Even in the face of adversity, trial and pain, we must never forget the capacity of our God to bring us through circumstances, to change our circumstances and to bring us into and through new and uncertain territory. Let God lead you throughout the year. Consecrate yourself to His service. Be prepared to get your feet wet and expect a miracle.

You are the God who performs miracles;
you display your power among the peoples.

Psalm 77:13-14 (NIV)

Allow the words of Isaiah 43:1-3 to saturate your very being:

The LORD who created you says, "Do not be afraid – I will save you. I have called you by name – you are mine. When you pass through deep waters, I will be with you; your troubles will not overwhelm you. When you pass through fire, you will not be burnt; the hard trials that come will not hurt you. For I am the LORD your God, the holy God of Israel who saves you ... You are precious to me. Do not be afraid – I am with you!"

Isaiah 43:1-3 (GNB)

7

Not on My Watch

I will stand at my watch and station myself on the ramparts; I will look to see what He will say to me.

Habakkuk 2:1 (NIVUK)

'Not on my watch!' is an English idiom meaning, 'That will not happen while I am on the lookout.' As regards the origin of the phrase, it is apparently a nautical expression and doesn't come from any specific incident but from the nature of command on board a ship; the day and night are divided into 'watches' (which are like shifts in industry) and the officers take turns to be 'officer of the watch', i.e. on duty and in charge.

In today's passage Habakkuk states, "I will stand at my watch and station myself ... I will look to see..." Are we positioned properly?

RMS Titanic was a British passenger liner that sank in the North Atlantic Ocean in the early morning of 15th April 1912 after colliding with an iceberg during her maiden voyage from Southampton to New York City. On 23rd October 2016, the headlines of a national newspaper read, "A rusty locker key from the doomed Titanic sells at auction for £85,000." It is thought to have fitted the locker that contained the crow's nest binoculars, vital in detecting threats to the liner lurking in the sea in the pre-sonar days of 1912. Catastrophically for the Titanic and the 1,522 lives lost with her, the key's owner, Second Officer David Blair, was removed from the crew at the last minute and in his haste forgot to hand it to his replacement. Without access to the binoculars, the lookouts in the crow's nest were forced to rely on their eyes and only saw the iceberg when it was too late to take action.

We must ensure that we are standing at our watch with our spiritual eyesight in place, our binoculars. Are we on the alert? Are we vigilant?

Pray diligently. Stay alert...

Colossians 4:2 (MSG)

Be sober-minded; be watchful.

1 Peter 5:8 (ESV)

With all prayer and petition pray at all times in the Spirit, and with this in view, be on the alert with all perseverance and petition for all the saints.

Ephesians 6:18 (NASB)

Be on the alert, stand firm in the faith, act like men, be strong.

1 Corinthians 16:13 (ESV)

In the words of Jesus:

"And what I say to you, I say to all: Watch!"

Mark 13:37 (NKJV)

8

Go in Peace

Let the peace of Christ [the inner calm of one who walks daily with Him] be the controlling factor in your hearts [deciding and settling questions that arise].

Colossians 3:15 (AMP)

What is peace? Peace is described here as "the inner calm of one who walks daily with Him." I continued to search the Scriptures to unearth the deeper meaning of "peace", or *eirene* as it is in the original Greek.

Luke 8:48 records the beautiful words of Jesus:

He said to her, "Daughter, your faith [your personal trust and confidence in Me] has made you well. Go in peace (untroubled, undisturbed well-being)."

Luke 8:48 (AMP)

Peace is "untroubled, undisturbed well-being".

Peter phrases it beautifully:

May grace (God's favour) and peace (which is perfect well-being, all necessary good, all spiritual prosperity, and freedom from fears and agitating passions and moral conflicts) be multiplied to you in [the full, personal, precise, and correct] knowledge of God and of Jesus our Lord.

2 Peter 1:2 (AMP)

Peace is "perfect well-being, all necessary good, all spiritual prosperity, and freedom from fears and agitating passions and moral conflicts."

In John 14 Jesus tenderly said:

"Peace I leave with you; My [perfect] peace I give to you; not as the world gives do I give to you. Do not let your heart be troubled, nor let it be afraid. [Let My perfect peace calm you in every

circumstance and give you courage and strength for every challenge.]"

John 14:27 (AMP)

Today may we allow His perfect peace to calm us in every circumstance and give us courage and strength for every challenge. May we know the inner calm of one who walks daily with Him. May we experience perfect well-being, all necessary good, all spiritual prosperity, and freedom from fears and agitating passions and moral conflicts. As Jesus said, "Go in peace. Go in untroubled, undisturbed well-being."

9

Get Wisdom

Get wisdom! Get understanding!

Proverbs 4:5 (NKJV)

*S*omeone shared the following quote with me on Facebook and it got me thinking about the topic of wisdom: "Knowledge is knowing that a tomato is a fruit. Wisdom is not putting it into the fruit bowl. Philosophy is wondering if that makes ketchup a smoothie!"

Proverbs 4:7 tells us:

Wisdom is the principal thing;
Therefore get wisdom.
And in all your getting, get understanding.

Proverbs 4:7 (NKJV)

In the previous chapter, Proverbs 3:13 says:

Happy is the man who finds wisdom
And the man who gets understanding.

Proverbs 3:13 (NKJV)

Later in chapter 24 we are told:

Through wisdom a house is built,
And through understanding it is established...

Proverbs 24:3

Sometimes in the Western mindset we merge the idea of knowledge and wisdom together without clear lines of demarcation. However, it is possible to be filled with knowledge and yet lack wisdom. So what is the difference? Knowledge is acquired information; wisdom is applied information. Wisdom lies not in the amount of knowledge acquired but in the degree of its application. Wisdom in general simply means the ability to apply the knowledge which we have obtained. We need knowledge.

My people are destroyed for lack of knowledge: because thou hast rejected knowledge.

Hosea 4:6 (KJV)

But we also need to apply the knowledge gained and translate it into living. As James put it in his letter, it is possible to be deficient in wisdom.

If any of you is deficient in wisdom, let him ask of the giving God [Who gives] to everyone liberally and ungrudgingly, without reproaching or faultfinding, and it will be given him. Only it must be in faith that he asks with no wavering (no hesitating, no doubting). For the one who wavers (hesitates, doubts) is like the billowing surge out at sea that is blown hither and thither and tossed by the wind.

James 1:5-6 (AMP)

Joshua shows us that by meditating on God's Word and applying it to our lives, we can deal wisely.

"You shall meditate on it day and night, that you may observe and do according to all that is written in it. For then you shall make your way prosperous, and then you shall deal wisely and have good success."

Joshua 1:8

May we all deal wisely and have good success today as we walk with the Lord.

10

The Power in Your Hand

Do not withhold good from those to whom it is due, when it is in your power to act. Do not say to your neighbour, "Come back tomorrow and I'll give it to you" – when you already have it with you.

Proverbs 3:27-28 (NIV)

The question was asked in Luke 10:29, "...who is my neighbour?"[36] The answer: *anyone who is in need.* We can talk about doctrine, theology and what we believe, but if our theology and beliefs do not have a direct impact upon how we live and relate to others then all of our talk is empty. John phrased it:

If anyone has material possessions and sees his brother in need but has no pity on him, how can the love of God be in him? Dear children, let us not love with words or tongue but with actions and in truth.

1 John 3:17-18 (NIVUK)

James states:

Suppose a brother or a sister is without clothes and daily food. If one of you says to them, "Go in peace; keep warm and well fed," but does nothing about their physical needs, what good is it?

James 2:15-16 (NIV)

If God had withheld good from us, where would we be?

A man fell into a pit and couldn't get himself out. People began to gather around and discuss the man, the pit and his predicament.

One subjective person yelled down to him, "I feel for you down there."

---

[36] NIVUK

An objective person stated the obvious: "It's logical that someone would fall down there."

A Pharisee scoffed, "Only bad people fall into pits."

A mathematician calculated how deep the pit was.

A news reporter wanted the exclusive story on the pit.

One self-centred person sobbed, "You haven't seen anything until you've seen my pit."

A fundamentalist screamed, "You deserve your pit."

A psychologist noted, "Your mother and father are to blame for your being in that pit."

An evasive person came along and avoided the subject of pits all together.

Then finally a man stepped from the crowd and walked to the pit, saying, "I also have been in a pit," and offering his hand, he pulled him out.

God's Word tells us:

He lifted me out of the pit of despair, out of the mud and the mire.
He set my feet on solid ground and steadied me as I walked along.
                                                        Psalm 40:2 (NLT)

Can we offer our hand to help someone today? It has been said, the smallest deed is better than the greatest intention.

11

The Power of Your Tongue

Death and life are in the power of the tongue,
And those who love it will eat its fruit.

Proverbs 18:21 (NKJV)

*I*s there really power in your words? Are they not simply sounds caused by air passing through your larynx? Do you ever think of the words you speak and the power they carry? Words do more than convey information. They have real power.

Notice that today's verse speaks of "the power of the tongue". It is obvious that the power referred to here is not the physical power of the tongue as a muscle, but the power of the words it produces. Words are a powerful force and the powerful effects of negative words cannot be underestimated. Sadly, many have been victims of verbal abuse. Words are weighty, powerful influencers. What will come out of your mouth today: death or life?

The tongue, even though it is among the smallest of all the members of the body[37] can do much damage. That's why Paul said to distance yourself from all corrupt communication.

Let no corrupting talk come out of your mouths, but only such as is good for building up, as fits the occasion, that it may give grace to those who hear.

Ephesians 4:29 (ESV)

James advised us to be "slow to speak":

Let everyone be quick to hear [be a careful, thoughtful listener], slow to speak [a speaker of carefully chosen words and], slow to anger [patient, reflective, forgiving].

James 1:19 (AMP)

---

[37] See James 3:5

Are you a speaker of carefully chosen words? Proverbs 13:3 tells us to guard our words.

Whoever guards his mouth preserves his life;
he who opens wide his lips comes to ruin.

Proverbs 13:3 (ESV)

Another proverb adds:

Whoever keeps his mouth and his tongue keeps himself out of trouble.

Proverbs 21:23 (ESV)

Still another praises the beneficial aspects of the tongue:

A word fitly spoken and in due season is like apples of gold in settings of silver.

Proverbs 25:11 (AMPC)

Proverbs 15:4 advises:

A gentle tongue [with its healing power] is a tree of life, but willful contrariness in it breaks down the spirit.

Proverbs 15:4 (AMPC)

Today, you can choose to make your mouth "a fountain of life"[38]. You can allow your words to bring healing. Your words can bring life to the weary. Determine to set an example in your speech.[39] Allow your words to make a difference.

---

[38] Proverbs 10:11
[39] See 1 Timothy 4:12

12

Great Expectations

In the morning, LORD, you hear my voice; in the morning I lay my requests before you and wait expectantly.

Psalm 5:3 (NIV)

*H*ave you ever read the literary classic *Great Expectations* written by Charles Dickens? I love that title *Great Expectations!* An important part of prayer is expectation and a fervent sense of expectancy. Whenever we pray, it should be with great expectation. Take the example of David in today's reading. When a need arose in his life, he laid out his requests in prayer and he looked to the Lord in expectation. Even in difficult circumstances he said:

But, O my soul, don't be discouraged. Don't be upset. Expect God to act! For I know that I shall again have plenty of reason to praise Him for all that He will do. He is my help! He is my God!

Psalm 42:11 (TLB)

Again, he declared:

My soul, wait thou only upon God; for my expectation is from Him.

Psalm 62:5 (KJV)

When we pray, we should expect to see the answer. Jesus said to us:

"...whatever things you ask when you pray, believe that you receive them, and you will have them."

Mark 11:24 (NKJV)

Again, He said:

"Ask, and it will be given you; seek, and you will find; knock, and it will be opened to you. For everyone who asks receives, and he who seeks finds, and to him who knocks it will be opened. Or what man is there among you who, if his sons asks for bread, will

give him a stone? Or if he asks for a fish, will he give him a serpent? If you then, being evil, know how to give good things to your children, how much more will your Father who is in heaven give good things to those who ask Him!"

Matthew 7:7-11 (NKJV)

Remember that there are no limits to what God can do because He is magnificent. Our confidence is in Him. I leave you to pause in His Presence and meditate on 1 John 5:14-15:

This is the confidence which we have before Him, that, if we ask anything according to His will, He hears us. And if we know that He hears us in whatever we ask, we know that we have the requests which we have asked from Him.

1 John 5:14-15 (NASB)

13

A Noisy Gong?

Let everything you do be done in love [motivated and inspired by God's love for us].

1 Corinthians 16:14 (AMP)

*P*aul encourages the church in Corinth to do everything "in love". Love is to regulate all that we do too. Without love we are nothing. Paul says:

Though I speak with the tongues of men and of angels, but have not love, I have become sounding brass or a clanging cymbal.

1 Corinthians 13:1 (NKJV)

He goes on to say:

If I have the gift of prophecy, and know all mysteries and all knowledge; and if I have all faith, so as to remove mountains, but do not have love, I am nothing.

1 Corinthians 13:2 (NASB)

Love is the key; love is the main thing.

Back in the first century, there was a large gong or cymbal hanging at the entrance of most pagan temples. When people came to worship, they hit the gong to awaken the pagan gods so that they would listen to their prayers. Here, Paul is saying that even if he were so blessed that he could speak with the greatest of eloquence in every language, but didn't have love, then his life was as useless as this ridiculous act of pounding on a gong to awaken non-existent gods.

Let everything you do be done in love. Love isn't merely emotion, love is motion. Love does. Love is a verb. John says:

But whoever has the world's goods (adequate resources), and sees his brother in need, but has no compassion for him, how does the love of God live in him?

1 John 3:17 (AMP)

Here is a clip of love in action:

Love suffers long and is kind; love does not envy; love does not parade itself, is not puffed up; does not behave rudely, does not seek its own, is not provoked, thinks no evil; does not rejoice in iniquity, but rejoices in the truth; bears all things, believes all things, hopes all things, endures all things.

1 Corinthians 13:4-6 (NKJV)

Jesus said to those who followed Him:

By this all will know that you are My disciples, if you have love for one another.

John 13:35 (NKJV)

How is this possible? "Let everything you do be done in love [motivated and inspired by God's love for us]." Here's my prayer: *Lord, teach me how to effectively, creatively, fully experience the conjugation of the verb 'love' in my life.*

14

It Is I

*But immediately He spoke to them, saying, "Take courage, it is I!
Do not be afraid!"*

Matthew 14:27 (AMP)

*T*he Jews, as well as the Romans, usually divided the night into four watches of three hours each. The first watch began at 6pm, the second at 9pm, the third at 12am and the fourth at 3am. It was during the fourth watch, between 3-6am, that Jesus came to His distressed disciples. Matthew 14:27 tells us of the encouraging voice of Jesus amid the storm:

*But immediately He spoke to them, saying, "Take courage, it is I!
Do not be afraid!"*

Matthew 14:27 (AMP)

Take courage. It is offered to you. Reach out and lay hold of it today. In Deuteronomy 31:6 Moses spoke:

*"Be strong. Take courage. Don't be intimidated. Don't give them
a second thought because God, your God, is striding ahead of you.
He's right there with you. He won't let you down; he won't leave
you."*

Deuteronomy 31:6 (MSG)

Psalm 27:14 tells us:

*Be strong and let your heart take courage; yes, wait for and
confidently expect the LORD.*

Psalm 27:14 (AMP)

Jesus said:

"These things I have spoken to you, so that in Me you may have peace. In the world you have tribulation, but take courage; I have overcome the world."

John 16:33 (NASB)

It is I. The words translated in our daily reading as "It is I" actually mean 'I AM'. This brings to mind God's self-identification to Moses. God said:

You shall tell the children of Israel this: 'I AM has sent me to you.'

Exodus 3:14 (WEB)

Jesus employed the same words in His declarations, "I am the way, the truth, the life;"[40] "I am the Good Shepherd,"[41] etc. When caught in the grip of unspeakable fear, unable to face what seems to lie ahead, it is precious to hear His voice saying, "It is I." Not merely, "I am here too," but, *"It is I."* Paul wrote in his very last epistle and in its very last chapter:

At my first defense no one supported me, but all deserted me; may it not be counted against them. But the Lord stood with me and strengthened me.

2 Timothy 4:16,17 (NASB)

Stop being afraid. Everyone feels afraid at some point in life whether it's a gnawing, anxious feeling or a paralysing phobia which freezes us into inaction. The Bible offers a powerful alternative to the voice of fear, reminding readers repeatedly, "Do not be afraid." Stop it! John wrote:

Perfect love casts out fear; for fear has torment.

1 John 4:18 (DARBY)

God has not given us a spirit of fear, but of power and of love and of a sound mind.

2 Timothy 1:7 (NKJV)

God tells us:

---

[40] Ref?
[41] Ref?

So do not fear, for I am with you; do not be dismayed, for I am your God. I will strengthen you and help you; I will uphold you with my righteous right hand.

Isaiah 41:10 (NIVUK)

The winds and waves of life may be adverse and threatening, but when anchored in Jesus Christ, we can hear His reassuring voice prompting us to take courage, reminding us of His Presence and convincing us to stop being afraid.

15

My Source of Courage, My Invincible Army

Though the fig tree does not blossom and there is no fruit on the vines, though the yield of the olive fails and the fields produce no food, though the flock is cut off from the fold and there are no cattle in the stalls, yet I will [choose to] rejoice in the Lord; I will [choose to] shout in exultation in the [victorious] God of my salvation! The Lord God is my strength [my source of courage, my invincible army]; He has made my feet [steady and sure] like hinds' feet and makes me walk [forward with spiritual confidence] on my high places [of challenge and responsibility].

Habakkuk 3:17-19 (AMPC)

Times were hard for Habakkuk and he asked God the two questions we often ask: "Why?" and "How long?" *Why are these things happening? How long will it be before they are rectified?* God answered him by revealing certain circumstances which must take place. Habakkuk realised that although he did not understand God's ways or timing, he could not doubt God's wisdom, love or reliability. That's when Habakkuk made the above declaration of faith. Even if everything that gave stability to his life crumbled, he would still trust the Lord, his true stability. Will you trust Him too? We can let the Devil point at negative circumstances in our life, and allow him to steal our joy, or we can individually declare:

Yet I will [choose to] rejoice in the Lord; I will [choose to] shout in exultation in the [victorious] God of my salvation! The Lord God is my strength [my source of courage, my invincible army].

Habakkuk 3:18 (AMPC)

What was it that allowed Habakkuk to rejoice in the Lord despite his circumstances? How can we do the same? Notice that Habakkuk doesn't just say, "Yet I will rejoice." The secret to his rejoicing is "...in the Lord."

That's the difference. Habakkuk knew his God and he knew that he was Saviour, Sovereign and strong.

The Sovereign LORD is my strength.

Habakkuk 3:19 (NIV)

He knew that God would strengthen him and enable him to endure the various trials. He knew that God would make him sure-footed when difficulties arose. He knew that God would save him and never fail him.

During World War I, the British soldier George Powell wrote a very famous song called *Pack Up Your Troubles in Your Old Kit Bag and Smile, Smile, Smile*. His brother Felix Powell was the one who made the song popular by setting it to music. The song said:

> *What's the use of worrying?*
> *It never was worthwhile.*
> *So, pack up your troubles*
> *In your old kit bag*
> *And smile, smile, smile.*

This song is said to have earned them about $60,000. Yet sadly, Felix Powell committed suicide during World War II in 1942, aged sixty-three. He shot himself in the heart while on guard duty, using his own rifle. Felix found himself unable to pack up his own troubles. He needed something greater than an "old kit bag"; he needed something stronger than a smile to hold him up when the storms of life came. Likewise, we need a Saviour who is sovereign and strong. Can you echo Habakkuk's words?

16

Always Having All Sufficiency in All Things

And God is able to make all grace abound to you, so that always having all sufficiency in everything, you may have an abundance for every good deed; as it is written, "He scattered abroad, he gave to the poor, His righteousness endures forever." Now He who supplies seed to the sower and bread for food will supply and multiply your seed for sowing and increase the harvest of your righteousness; you will be enriched in everything for all liberality, which through us is producing thanksgiving to God. For the ministry of this service is not only fully supplying the needs of the saints, but is also overflowing through many thanksgivings to God.

2 Corinthians 9:8-12 (NASB)

Do you believe the truth of these verses?

- God is able to make all grace abound to you. He wants to impact your life with every aspect of His grace.
- You will always have all sufficiency in everything.
- You will have an abundance for every good deed.
- He will supply and multiply your seed for sowing.
- He will increase the harvest of your righteousness.
- You will be enriched in everything for all liberality.
- This will result in thanksgiving to God.

The literal Greek expression is 'in all things always, all' (*panti pantote pasan*) or 'in everything always all self-sufficiency'. God is able to give all grace, all sufficiency, for all things, for every good work. Do not settle for the limitations of *some* when God is offering you *all*. Notice that it is *for every good work*. It is not for carnal indulgence. It is not for subsidising our luxuries or for hoarding. It is for enriching others and supplying the needs of the saints.

There is one who scatters, and yet increases all the more, and there is one who withholds what is justly due, and yet it results only in want. The generous man will be prosperous, and he who waters will himself be watered.

Proverbs 11:24-25 (NASB)

May we live as faithful stewards bringing thanksgiving and glory to God. He is the Giver of every good and perfect gift.

17

Merci for Mercies

The steadfast love of the LORD never ceases;
his mercies never come to an end;
they are new every morning;
great is Your faithfulness.

Lamentations 3:22-23 (ESV)

What is your first thought upon waking in the morning? If you're like a lot of people, it might be one of resistance. You don't want to get out from under the duvet. You don't feel like facing your to-do list. You don't want to go to that meeting. You're not exactly enthused about struggling through another routine day.

Or maybe your attitude is the opposite. *What a privilege it is to be alive! I am blessed with fresh air, the fragrance of nature, friends and loved ones, food and shelter, the ability to laugh and create and imagine. I am blessed with God's promises and His tender mercies.*

In the book of Lamentations, Jeremiah talked about waking up each day under the blanket of God's tender mercies. His mercies never come to an end; they are new every morning. The Hebrew word translated here as 'mercies' is used 248 times in the Old Testament. It is a sweeping, all-inclusive term to describe God's love, goodness, kindness, faithfulness, forgiveness and compassion.

In 2 Corinthians 1:3 God is called "the Father of mercies"[42]. We are told in Psalm 103:3-4 that God "redeemeth thy life from destruction; who crowneth thee with lovingkindness and tender mercies"[43].

Our heavenly Father is always merciful. The Bible even calls His throne "the throne of grace [where] we may receive mercy and find grace to help in time of need"[44]. Our proper response to God's mercy toward

---

[42] AMP
[43] KJV
[44] Hebrews 4:16 (NASB)

113

us is not only to acknowledge and embrace it but to offer ourselves fully to Him.

> *I therefore urge you, brothers, in view of God's mercies, to offer your bodies as living sacrifices that are holy and pleasing to God, for this is the reasonable way for you to worship.*
>
> Romans 12:1 (ISV)

Go ahead, thank God for His tender mercies today. Merci for mercies.

18

You Follow Me

Peter ... said to Jesus, "But Lord, what about this man?"
Jesus said to him, "...what is that to you? You follow Me."

John 21:21-22 (NKJV)

*I*n the preceding verses, Peter received new direction for his life. He was instructed to feed the Lord's people. He was given the ministry of leadership in the early church. He was restored to the place of service and told that he would serve the Lord for many years, and that even in His death, he would glorify God. When Peter learns of this, he then asks Jesus about John. Jesus responds by telling Peter to tend to his own life and the Lord will take care of John.

Peter's mind seems to have been distracted from the command to follow the Saviour by a very simple incident. "Turning his head"[45], it is said, he saw John following – and the sight of his fellow disciple awakened his curiosity and he made his speculative inquiry. *Will John have a similar commission? What is your plan for his life? Will it be easier than mine? Will it be harder than mine? Will it be about the same? Will he be more successful?* Sometimes we can be easily distracted by what others are doing. We think God's plan for their life is better than His plan for ours. But God's plan for each of us is the same: follow Jesus. When we watch Him intently, we'll not be distracted by God's plan for anyone else.

"Follow me" is the most oft-repeated command of Jesus in all the Gospels. The word for "follow" is worth pondering. It is the Greek word *akoloutheo*. It means:

- to follow one who precedes;
- to join him as his attendant;
- to side with his party;

---

[45] John 21:21 (MSG)

- to walk the same road.

It signifies obedience, the kind of obedience a soldier gives his commanding officer. It signifies commitment, the kind of commitment which is unflinching and unwavering. It signifies loyalty, the kind of loyalty which is willing to surrender all for a great cause.

When Jesus found Peter and called him the first time, this was His command – "Follow Me."[46] When he recommissions Peter, He issues the same call. But in between we read that "Peter followed Him afar off":

> *But Peter followed Him afar off unto the high priest's palace, and went in, and sat with the servants, to see the end.*
>
> *Matthew 26:58 (KJV)*

He was no longer by the Lord's side with courage. He had fallen back and was looking on from afar. He had distanced himself from Christ, and this was the beginning of his downfall. Jesus says to each of us, "Follow Me." Don't be distracted by what others are doing. Don't distance yourself from the Lord. He says, " *You* follow Me."

---

[46] Matthew 4:19 (NKJV)

19

No Turning Back

The children of Ephraim, being armed, and carrying bows, turned back in the day of battle.

Psalm 78:9

Featuring prominently on the Australian Coat of Arms are two of Australia's most iconic animals – the kangaroo and emu – leading to a common trivia question: why them and not the koala, wombat or echidna? It's commonly believed that the reason why they are on the Coat of Arms is because they are the two animals that are unable to walk backwards, signifying the aspiration and intent of the nation to always move forwards.

In today's verse the "children of Ephraim" are described as "being armed, and carrying bows". Psalms 78 chronicles the work which the Lord has done throughout the history of Israel – the many times He saved them, the miracles, the crossing of the Red Sea, the water from rocks in the desert, the manna from heaven, and His mercy shown a thousand times over again. Yet the men of Ephraim, though armed with bows, turned back on the day of battle, forgetting all that God had done, the marvellous deeds He had performed. As soon as life became difficult, they retreated and left; they forsook their obedience to the Lord who had saved them. Is there a battle you're facing today? God expects us to stand against the enemy, not retreat!

Wherefore take unto you the whole armour of God, that ye may be able to withstand in the evil day, and having done all, to stand.

Ephesians 6:13 (KJV)

In the description of the Christian's armour, there is no mention of protection for the back – we are expected to stand against the enemy, not turn back or run away.

When Julius Caesar landed on the shores of Britain with his Roman legions, he took a bold and decisive step to ensure the success of his military venture. Ordering his men to march to the edge of the Cliffs of Dover, he commanded them to look down at the water below. To their amazement, they saw every ship in which they had crossed the channel engulfed in flames. Caesar had deliberately cut off any possibility of retreat. Now that his soldiers were unable to return to the continent, there was nothing left for them to do but to advance and conquer. And that is exactly what they did. Let's have the same mindset: *advance*. As the book of Hebrews says:

> *Now the just shall live by faith: but if any man draw back, my soul shall have no pleasure in him. But we are not of them who draw back unto perdition; but of them that believe to the saving of the soul.*
>
> Hebrews 10:38-39 (KJV)

20

V-Formation

Let us hold unswervingly to the hope we profess, for he who promised is faithful. And let us consider how we may spur one another on toward love and good deeds, not giving up meeting together, as some are in the habit of doing, but encouraging one another – and all the more as you see the Day approaching.

Hebrews 10:23-25 (NIVUK)

Look up into the sky and you will probably observe the occasional bird flying overhead. At certain times of year you may even spot some of the migratory kind making epic journeys. Something that has always intrigued me is the genius of migration and the amazing way geese fly in their characteristic V-formation. Research has shown why they choose to adopt this particular formation. The aerodynamic V shape reduces the air drag which each bird experiences when in flight in comparison to a bird flying solo. This allows them to cover longer distances with much less effort. In fact, by flying in a V-formation, the whole flock adds 71% more flying range than if each bird flew alone. This technique is now employed as a basic flight formation for military aircraft and professional cycling races.

This is amazing but there is more to learn from the migratory geese. When the lead goose gets tired, it rotates back into the formation and another goose flies at the point position. This cycle continues as they travel to their destination and in this way, they minimise the onset of fatigue. As they fly, the geese honk to recognise each other and encourage those up front to keep up their speed. When a goose gets sick or wounded, two geese drop out of formation and follow it down to help and protect it. They stay with it until it dies or is able to fly again. They share a common goal, achieve more together, offer support in challenging times and encourage one another. They remind me of 1 Corinthians 3:9:

For we are fellow workmen (joint promoters, labourers together) with and for God.

1 Corinthians 3:9 (AMP)

As fellow workmen we too share a common goal and must hold unswervingly to the hope we profess. We too should spur one another on and be supportive of one another. We too should honk a word of encouragement. The New Testament is replete with references about how we are to love, support and encourage one another. Why not take some time to look up the "one another" passages in the New Testament[47] – they provide a useful study. Together we can make a difference.

---

[47] e.g. *www.biblegateway.com/quicksearch/?quicksearch="one+another"*

21

V-Formation

And we know that God causes all things to work together for good to those who love God, to those who are called according to His purpose.

Romans 8:28 (NASB)

*I*t's one thing after another! It's just one of those things. To be in the thick of things. These are common idioms which work their way into daily dialogue. We like to refer to "things" in a rather unspecified way. Paul also mentions multiple "things":

And we know that God causes all things to work together for good to those who love God, to those who are called according to His purpose. ... What then shall we say to these things? If God is for us, who is against us? He who did not spare His own Son, but delivered Him over for us all, how will He not also with Him freely give us all things? But in all these things we overwhelmingly conquer through Him who loved us. For I am convinced that neither death, nor life, nor angels, nor principalities, nor things present, nor things to come, nor powers, nor height, nor depth, nor any other created thing, will be able to separate us from the love of God, which is in Christ Jesus our Lord.

Romans 8:28-32,37-39 (NASB)

"All *things* to work together for good ... What then shall we say to these *things*? ... Will He not also with Him freely give us all *things*? ... But in all these *things* we overwhelmingly conquer..."

Let's look at verse 28: "We know that God causes all things to work together for good to those who love God..." This speaks of certainty: "We *know*..." Paul does not say, "We think..." or, "We hope..." The verse also speaks of completeness: "all things". Not *most*, not *some*, but *all*. It speaks of cause: "God *causes* all things to work together for good." He is in control of both the painful and the pleasant experiences of life and has an eternal purpose in mind. It is difficult for anyone to orchestrate several different events at one time – try patting your head and rubbing your stomach at the same time. But God controls all of the events in the life of every believer. Joseph said:

> *Even though you planned evil against me, God planned good to come out of it. This was to keep many people alive, as he is doing now.*

Genesis 50:20 (GW)

Paul said that we are "more than conquerors" "in all these things". Most of us have the idea that victory occurs when we are living lives that are free from troubles, afflictions and heartaches. But Paul tells us that "in all *these things* we overwhelmingly conquer through Him who loved us".

What are "these things"? "Tribulation, or distress, or persecution, or famine, or nakedness, or peril, or sword." Tribulation is to be squeezed or to feel pressure. Distress is literally 'a narrow place'. It means to be hemmed in by one's circumstances. Persecution is suffering inflicted on us because of our relationship with Jesus. Famine is a lack of necessary resources. Nakedness is a lack of proper clothing. Peril is the threat of imminent danger. Sword is the threat of murder. Paul tells us that in or amid all these things, we "are" (present tense) more than conquerors and the only reason that we are victorious is "through Him that loved us". It is not circumstantial. It is relational. So, how're things going?

22

And Jesus Stopped

*Then they came to Jericho. And as He was leaving Jericho with
His disciples and a large crowd, a blind beggar named Bartimaeus,
the son of Timaeus, was sitting by the road. When he heard that
it was Jesus the Nazarene, he began to cry out and say, "Jesus,
Son of David, have mercy on me!" Many were sternly telling him
to be quiet, but he kept crying out all the more, "Son of David,
have mercy on me!" And Jesus stopped and said, "Call him here."
So they called the blind man, saying to him, "Take courage, stand
up! He is calling for you." Throwing aside his cloak, he jumped
up and came to Jesus. And answering him, Jesus said, "What do
you want Me to do for you?" And the blind man said to Him,
"Rabboni, I want to regain my sight!" And Jesus said to him,
"Go; your faith has made you well." Immediately he regained his
sight and began following Him on the road.*

Mark 10:46-52 (NASB)

Verse 49 says, "And Jesus stopped." Or, "Jesus stopped in His
tracks." Let's remember that He was on a mission. He was
determined. He had a goal in mind. He set His face to go to
Jerusalem. But even while He was moving with determination toward
Jerusalem, He was still interruptible. Here we read that Jesus stopped
because of the desperate cry of one person. One individual. Jesus, the
most important person, during the most important week in history,
stopped. He did not shun the interruption, He honoured it. How do we
respond to the cries for help from people in our tracks? People are not
obstacles to avoid or sidestep. Every person has a story and every person
is valuable in God's sight. We are to respond to the people God puts in
our path, remembering that ministering to them is ministering to Him.

Jesus said in Matthew 25:

*"Then the King will say to those on His right, 'Come, you who
are blessed of My Father, inherit the kingdom prepared for you*

from the foundation of the world. For I was hungry, and you gave Me something to eat; I was thirsty, and you gave Me something to drink; I was a stranger, and you invited Me in; naked, and you clothed Me; I was sick, and you visited Me; I was in prison, and you came to Me.' Then the righteous will answer Him, 'Lord, when did we see You hungry, and feed You, or thirsty, and give You something to drink? And when did we see You a stranger, and invite You in, or naked, and clothe You? When did we see You sick, or in prison, and come to You?' The King will answer and say to them, 'Truly I say to you, to the extent that you did it to one of these brothers of Mine, even the least of them, you did it to Me.'"

Matthew 25:34-40 (NASB)

We know Jesus was in great demand, but He greeted interruptions as opportunities, trusting them as divine appointments. Think of this: most of Jesus' miracles were interruptions. Often He was on the way to another appointment when someone else would stop Him and provide Him the opportunity to do something miraculous. Sometimes where we are going isn't as important as who we'll meet on the way. There is so much pain and loneliness in the world, you can be sure that the person next to you on the bus or the checkout at the grocery store could use a kind word, a smile or a helping hand. Get off your mobile phone and talk to them. Ask them how their day is going and mean it. Connect with the people around you.

23

Be My Witness

But you will receive power when the Holy Spirit has come upon you; and you shall be My witnesses both in Jerusalem, and in all Judea and Samaria, and even to the remotest part of the earth.

Acts 1:8 (ESV)

*J*ust before He returned to heaven, Jesus explained to His disciples what they were to do after His departure. What He said to them, He also says to us: "....you will receive power..." Every believer is commissioned, commanded and compelled to share the gospel with a lost world. "You" refers to the faithful men and women who live ordinary lives in the world, attending school, making a living, raising families, participating in the daily life of our community.

"...be My witnesses..." The word "witness" translates the Greek word *martus*. It has a legal meaning: 'to affirm that one has seen or heard or experienced something'. A witness in a trial is called upon to tell what they have seen and what they know to be true. He or she is 'one who furnishes evidence'. A witness is someone who can say, "I know this is true." A witness is called on to tell the truth, the whole truth and nothing but the truth. Jesus is the way, the truth and the life. He is the only hope the world has for salvation.[48] He said that we are witnesses "unto Me"[49] or "My witnesses". *Martus* also gives us the English word 'martyr', the same word used of Stephen when he was stoned, the ultimate sacrifice for the spreading of the good news.

"Unto the uttermost part of the earth"[50]. The Greek word for "uttermost" refers to the extremities of the earth. It means that we must take the gospel to every nook and cranny of the globe. There are still many people groups without any Christian witness. Most of us will never

---

[48] See John 14:6; Acts 4:12; Acts 16:31.
[49] KJV
[50] KJV

go to "the uttermost part of the earth" but we can pray and support those who do. From our knees we can impact distant lands and enter closed nations.

> *[Let us] tell of His glory among the nations, His wonderful deeds among all the peoples. For great is the LORD, and greatly to be praised.*
>
> *1 Chronicles 16:24-25 (NASB)*

24

Oh, That...

Oh, that You would rend the heavens and come down, that the mountains might quake at Your presence – as fire kindles the brushwood, as fire causes water to boil – to make Your name known to Your adversaries, that the nations may tremble at Your presence!

Isaiah 64:1-2 (NASB)

The prophet's words are intense and intentional here. Is there an "Oh, that..." in our praying? Is there an intensity? Is there a passion, a longing, a burden, tears and concern? Are we just *saying* prayers or are we really *praying*? The prophet knew that God was the answer and so he directly addressed God, "Oh, that You would..." Revival is always the sovereign act of God. It is the Lord God rending the heavens and coming down among His people.[51] In other words, revival is a mighty manifestation of the presence and power of God. If you would have asked the recipients of past revivals what happened, they would have said, "The Lord came down among us and we were overwhelmed with the sense of His presence and power." That is what happened in the Ulster revival of 1859, in the valleys of Wales in 1904 and in the Scottish Hebrides.

Is there a longing in our hearts to see the mountains melt – mountains of pride, rebellion, division, deception and every obstacle to God's work? Is there a longing to see the nations tremble at the undeniable Presence of God and stand in awe of Him? To quote from an extract given by the parish minister of Barvas in Scotland:

You could feel His presence in the homes of the people, on meadow and moor land, and even on the public roads.

---

[51] See Isaiah 64:1

Can you identify with the cry from the heart of Isaiah the prophet? Is this your cry, too? As we pray may there be an "Oh that..." in our prayers to the glory of God.

25

Tender and Compassionate

Are your hearts tender and compassionate? Then make me truly happy by agreeing wholeheartedly with each other, loving one another, and working together with one mind and purpose. Don't be selfish; don't try to impress others. Be humble, thinking of others as better than yourselves. Don't look out only for your own interests, but take an interest in others, too. You must have the same attitude that Christ Jesus had.

Philippians 2:1-5 (NLT)

If there be therefore any consolation in Christ, if any comfort of love, if any fellowship of the Spirit, if any bowels and mercies, fulfil ye my joy, that ye be likeminded.

Philippians 2:1-2 (KJV)

Are our hearts "tender and compassionate"? As we see in the King James Version, it is also rendered, "...if any bowels and mercies..." The Greek word for showing compassion is *splagchnizomai* which means 'to be moved in the inward parts' or 'to be gut-wrenching' i.e. 'to feel compassion'. The inward organs were considered the seat of emotion and intention and so it described the compassion which moves a man to the deepest depths of his being.

Be kind to one another, tenderhearted, forgiving one another, as God in Christ forgave you.

Ephesians 4:32 (NKJV)

Finally, all of you, have unity of mind, sympathy, brotherly love, a tender heart, and a humble mind.

1 Peter 3:8 (ESVUK)

Jesus is our example in compassion:

When He saw the crowds, He had compassion for them, because they were harassed and helpless, like sheep without a shepherd.

Matthew 9:36 (ESVUK)

And Jesus went forth, and saw a great multitude, and was moved with compassion toward them, and he healed their sick.

Matthew 14:14 (KJV)

Are we "moved with compassion"? The phrase means 'stirred to action'. Jesus didn't just sit back and notice the needs of the people. He was moved and stirred in His heart. He felt their pain. There was more than an awareness of their situation; there was action.

Beloved children, our love can't be an abstract theory we only talk about, but a way of life demonstrated through our loving deeds.

1 John 3:18 (TPT)

Compassion is actually something we are to put on and wear:

Therefore, as God's chosen people, holy and dearly loved, clothe yourselves with compassion, kindness, humility, gentleness and patience.

Colossians 3:12 (NIVUK)

As we go about today, let's make sure that our hearts are tender and compassionate.

26

Station Yourselves

You need not fight in this battle; station yourselves, stand and see
the salvation of the LORD on your behalf, O Judah and Jerusalem.

2 Chronicles 20:17 (NASB)

*J*ehoshaphat was shaken one morning when his intelligence sources came running in with horrifying news: "A great multitude is coming against you from beyond the sea, from Syria; and they are in Hazazon Tamar."[52] In reality this meant that the enemy coalition was about 15 miles south of Jerusalem, on the western shore of the Dead Sea. Jehoshaphat's life and his entire kingdom were on the brink of extinction. So what did he do?

Let's put ourselves in Jehoshaphat's place. What would we do if we heard some threatening news that affected our future and maybe our lives? Verse three records the response of Jehoshaphat:

Jehoshaphat ... turned his attention to seek the LORD.

2 Chronicles 20:3 (NASB)

Jehoshaphat said, "Let's pray and seek the direction of God." His prayer is recorded in verses 6-12. In the first four verses His focus is on God Himself; in the last three verses, he mentions the problem. This godly king did the right thing: he encouraged the people to trust God in the face of this overwhelming crisis. In prayer he declared:

"For we are powerless before this great multitude who are coming
against us; nor do we know what to do, but our eyes are on You."

2 Chronicles 20:12 (NASB)

It was then recorded that "the Spirit of the LORD came upon Jahaziel"[53] the prophet, who said:

---

[52] 2 Chronicles 20:1-2 (NKJV)
[53] 2 Chronicles 20:14 (NASB)

"Do not fear or be dismayed because of this great multitude, for the battle is not yours but God's."

2 Chronicles 20:15 (NASB)

He continued:

"You need not fight in this battle; station yourselves, stand and see the salvation of the LORD on your behalf..."

2 Chronicles 20:17 (NASB)

God confused the enemy and the very place of battle became a place of blessings – *Berakah*. Do you feel as if there is a multitude rising up against you? Perhaps you too are saying, "I do not know what to do." If so, don't be afraid. Instead, seek the Lord and 'station' yourself. Station yourself in prayer; stand and see the salvation of the Lord on your behalf.

27

Sunergos

What then is Apollos? And what is Paul? Servants through whom you believed, even as the Lord gave opportunity to each one. I planted, Apollos watered, but God was causing the growth. So then neither the one who plants nor the one who waters is anything, but God who causes the growth. Now he who plants and he who waters are one; but each will receive his own reward according to his own labour. For we are God's fellow workers; you are God's field, God's building.

1 Corinthians 3:5-9 (NASB)

*S*ome Christians put their leaders on pedestals and then bemoan the fact that they have feet of clay. We see this happening in Corinth concerning Apollos and Paul. Paul had to remind the people that they were simply servants and that the focus must be on God.

Sunergos is the New Testament word literally meaning 'a companion in work', 'fellow worker' or 'partner'. You find it in 1 Corinthians 3:9:

For we are labourers together with God...

1 Corinthians 3:9 (KJV)

The Amplified Bible says:

For we are fellow workmen (joint promoters, labourers together) with and for God.

1 Corinthians 3:5-9 (AMPC)

What a privilege to share in God's work. In the realm of sports today and even in the corporate world, we often hear the terms 'team player', 'team effort'. What a joy it is to be a team player united in a common purpose concerning the Kingdom of God. The word *sunergos* is where is get our English word 'synergy'. The Oxford Dictionary defines 'synergy' as "the interaction or cooperation of two or more organisations, substances, or other agents to produce a combined effect greater than the sum of their separate effects". We are all servants, labourers together with God. That puts the supernatural with the *sunergos*. No wonder the verb *sunergeo* translated as "work with" appears in Mark 16:20:

> *And they went out and preached everywhere, while the Lord worked with them, and confirmed the word by the signs that followed.*
>
> Mark 16:20 (NASB)

Keep planting, keep watering, keep working, keep praying, and as you do, know that the Lord is working with you.

28

Be a Berean

The brethren immediately sent Paul and Silas away by night to Berea, and when they arrived, they went into the synagogue of the Jews. Now these were more noble-minded than those in Thessalonica, for they received the word with great eagerness, examining the Scriptures daily to see whether these things were so.

Acts 17:10-11 (NASB)

Who were the Bereans in the Bible? They were residents of the city of Berea in Macedonia. Paul and Silas preached to them during Paul's second missionary journey. The Bereans were commended because they exhibited several positive characteristics:

- They were called noble-minded / open to seeking truth / teachable / not prejudiced.
- They received the Word with great eagerness.
- They examined the Scriptures daily.

The Bereans wanted to know the Truth. They did not settle for sermons that were based on shoddy exegesis or emotionalism. Scripture was their accurate and effective filter for receiving truth and rejecting error. There is no mention of the Bereans consulting with any sources other than Scripture. Their belief in the sufficiency of Scripture is evident by their use of it as the sole, necessary plumb line of truth. Modern wolves now roam among God's flock in sophisticated sheepskins. The seriousness of such a threat demands that we be present-day Bereans. Do not just take what your favourite preacher or speaker or author or blogger says at face value. Make sure it lines up with the Scriptures. The Word of God is the only absolute we have; all teaching must be checked against this absolute standard. Paul tells us to "examine everything carefully; hold fast to that which is good"[54]. Jesus tell us:

> *"If you abide in My word, you are My disciples indeed. And you shall know the truth, and the truth shall make you free."*
>
> *John 8:31-32 (NKJV)*

Let us commit to examining the Scriptures daily and embracing the truth.

---

[54] 1 Thessalonians 5:21 (NASB)

29

Dog or Cat Mentality?

Seek and deeply long for His face and His presence continually.

Psalm 105:4 (AMP)

For many years dog and cat owners have been bickering over the relative merits of each type of pet. But in recent years, scientific researchers have started to weigh in – and most of their findings so far come down firmly on the side of dogs. Research has revealed that cats can be a little self-serving, a touch self-centred, aloof, manipulative and they don't seem to have the same sort of emotional attachment to their owners. It's been said that they meet the Oxford Dictionary's definition of selfish: being "concerned chiefly with one's own personal profit or pleasure". On the other hand, many of the qualities which come effortlessly to dogs are a sense of loyalty to its owner, unconditional love, selflessness and unflagging optimism.

I was thinking of this as I considered our relationship with God. The Bible says:

Seek and deeply long for His face and His presence continually.

Psalm 105:4 (AMP)

You will seek me and find me when you seek me with all your heart.

Jeremiah 29:13 (ESV)

What are our motives in seeking God? Applying the above 'catlike' mentality, are we purely seeking Him for selfish reasons, devoid of emotional attachment? Are we materialistic, treating God like a cosmic slot machine that yields desired rewards when presented with the right combination of words? Or, are we like a dog and seeking Him with no hidden agenda? Are we praying for only our needs and comfort or for global impact? Is it all about me or all about Him? David said:

When You said, "Seek My face,"
My heart said to You, "Your face, LORD, I will seek."

Psalm 27:8 (NKJV)

Let's seek Him with selfless devotion considering it a privilege to be in His presence.

30

Who is Adequate for These Things?

But thanks be to God, who always leads us in triumph in Christ, and manifests through us the sweet aroma of the knowledge of Him in every place. For we are a fragrance of Christ to God among those who are being saved and among those who are perishing; to the one an aroma from death to death, to the other an aroma from life to life. And who is adequate for these things?

2 Corinthians 2:14-16 (NASB)

Who is adequate for these things? That's the question asked in 2 Corinthians 2. Does Paul's cry here resonate in your heart? In light of such responsibility, are you confronted with the reality of your own utter inadequacy? When you think of what you are sent to do, I am sure that is a question that grips your heart as it does mine. *Who can do this?* It is very easy to get overwhelmed by the magnitude of the task, especially when we consider the Great Commission. *Who is sufficient for these things?*

What is the answer to this question? Paul goes on to answer it in the third chapter:

Not that we are adequate in ourselves to consider anything as coming from ourselves, but our adequacy is from God, who also made us adequate as servants of a new covenant.

2 Corinthians 3:5-6 (NASB)

To use the language of 2 Corinthians 4:7, He transports the treasure of the gospel in unimpressive, weak earthen vessels. Why?

...so that the surpassing greatness of the power will be of God and not from ourselves...

2 Corinthians 4:7 (NASB)

Our adequacy is from God. The word "adequate" in the original Greek is *hikanos* meaning 'sufficient, competent, able and qualified'. We ourselves are of no account, and what we can do is likewise of no account. But the sufficiency, competency and qualification for the ministry comes from the living God Himself. God has graciously equipped us as sufficient to dispense and disperse the sweet fragrance of Christ to a lost and dying world. Remember this: apart from Christ, we can do nothing.[55] On the other hand, with Christ we are adequate for all things.

I can do all things through Christ who strengthens me.

Philippians 4:13 (NKJV)

---

[55] See John 15:5

31

Your Petition Has Been Heard

But the angel said to him, "Do not be afraid, Zacharias, for your petition has been heard, and your wife Elizabeth will bear you a son, and you will give him the name John."

Luke 1:13 (NKJV)

To put today's verse in context, I recommend reading Luke 1:5-14. Elizabeth was barren, and she and Zacharias were both elderly. They had prayed for a son but it seemed that their prayer had seemingly gone unnoticed. What seemed like unexplainable silence was really God's work of preparing them for this incredible day. God wasn't late. God knew the exact time that Jesus would be born – "[in] the fullness of time"[56]. God knew exactly when He would need to send a forerunner (John the Baptist) to prepare the way. The age or physical condition of Zacharias and Elizabeth were no obstacle at all.

What have you been praying for? I encourage you right now to stand in faith for the answer. God's delays are not God's denials. His Word says:

Call to Me, and I will answer you, and show you great and mighty things...

Jeremiah 33:3 (NKJV)

He shall call upon Me, and I will answer him;
I will be with him in trouble;
I will deliver him and honor him.

Psalm 91:15 (NKJV)

Jesus stated:

---

[56] Galatians 4:4 (ESV)

"Therefore I tell you, whatever you ask in prayer, believe that you have received it, and it will be yours."

Mark 11:24 (ESVUK)

Hebrews 4 invites us:

Let us then fearlessly and confidently and boldly draw near to the throne of grace (the throne of God's unmerited favour), that we may receive mercy [for our failures] and find grace to help in good time for every need [appropriate help and well-timed help, coming just when we need it].

Hebrews 4:16 (AMP)

Do not be afraid, for your petition has been heard.

February

February

1

I Want to See a Mighty Flood of Justice

Take away from Me the noise of your songs; I will not even listen to the sound of your harps. But let justice roll down like waters and righteousness like an ever-flowing stream.

Amos 5:23-24 (NASB)

The words of Amos were meant to shock. He was confrontational and controversial. Wouldn't we be shocked if God said, "I'm tired of listening to your prayers. All of your hymns, anthems and songs sound out of tune to me." As The Living Bible translates it:

Away with your hymns of praise – they are mere noise to my ears. I will not listen to your music, no matter how lovely it is. I want to see a mighty flood of justice – a torrent of doing good.

Amos 5:23-24 (TLB)

Amos voices prophetic rage against the injustices of the day. If he were alive today, what might he say?

I want to see a mighty flood of justice, an endless river of righteous living.

Amos 5:24 (NLT)

Justice is equated with righteous living. Amos throws out a challenge: do our words and actions in worship and in prayer line up with justice and righteousness in our daily life? He goes on to say:

Seek good and not evil, that you may live;
And thus may the LORD God of hosts be with you,
Just as you have said!
Hate evil, love good,
And establish justice in the gate!

Perhaps the LORD God of hosts
May be gracious to the remnant of Joseph.

Amos 5:14-15 (NASB)

Like the other prophets – Isaiah, Micah and Hosea – we are called to concrete actions in the way we each live our lives; we are called to do justice, love kindness and walk humbly with God. The Hebrew word translated as "justice" has to do with right order in society, especially related to the poor and the weak. We have to read the rest of Amos to find out the specifics of what God is upset about. To generalise, God is upset with how the powerful are treating the powerless. The rich are getting richer while the poor are getting poorer. They are doing nothing for the widow and orphan who have no protection. They are doing nothing for the poor who have no food. They are doing nothing for the foreigners who are locked out of society. In selfishness they "turned justice into wormwood, and [laid] righteousness to rest in the earth"[57]. There was worship on the Sabbath but cheating in business on Monday. There was prayer on the Sabbath but oppressing the poor on Monday. What a contrast to the way we should live.

Let's obediently accept and honour the words of Amos 5:24 and truly worship the God of justice.

But let justice roll down like waters and righteousness like an ever-flowing stream.

Amos 5:24 (NASB)

---

[57] Amos 5:7 (NKJV)

2

The Riches of God's Word

The law of the LORD is perfect, restoring the soul;
The testimony of the LORD is sure, making wise the simple.
The precepts of the LORD are right, rejoicing the heart;
The commandment of the LORD is pure, enlightening the eyes.

Psalm 19:7-8 (NASB)

How important is God's Word to you? It is said that when the famous missionary Dr. David Livingstone started his trek across Africa he had 73 books in three packs, weighing 180 pounds. After the party had gone 300 miles, Livingstone was obliged to throw away some of the books because of the fatigue of those carrying his baggage. As he continued on his journey his library grew smaller and smaller, until he had but one book left: his Bible. Why did he keep his Bible? Psalm 19 holds the clues. In Psalm 19, David shows that God has spoken to us through His revelation in His handiwork[58] and in His handwriting[59]. David uses many ways to describe God's Word in this psalm, such as perfect, trustworthy, right, precious etc. He also tells us of its benefits in verses 7-8:

- The instructions of the Lord are perfect, reviving the soul.
- The decrees of the Lord are trustworthy, making wise the simple.
- The commandments of the Lord are right, bringing joy to the heart.
- The commands of the Lord are clear, giving insight for living.

"Reviving the soul ... making wise the simple ... bringing joy to the heart ... giving insight for living..."[60]

---

[58] Psalm 19:1-6
[59] Psalm 19:7-11
[60] Verses / version???

Reading and heeding God's Word brings life to our souls. "The words that I speak to you," Jesus said, "are spirit, and they are life."[61] David used the same word in Psalm 23 when he said:

He restores my soul;
He guides me in the paths of righteousness
For His name's sake.

Psalm 23:3 (NASB)

Reading and heeding God's Word makes us wise. We can become wise through the revelation of Holy Scripture. David said in Psalm 119:

Your commandments make me wiser than my enemies...

Psalm 119:98 (AMP)

Wisdom is the ability to respond correctly to life's situations. The wisdom from God's Word shows us how our infinitely wise Creator has ordained for us to live.

The unfolding of Your words gives light;
It gives understanding to the simple.

Psalm 119:130 (NASB)

Reading and heeding God's Word brings joy to our hearts. It's good news of great joy.

When your words came, I ate them; they were my joy and my heart's delight...

Jeremiah 15:16 (NIVUK)

Strong's Concordance tells us that the word for "ate" literally means 'to devour'. This reflects Jeremiah's avid hunger for God's Word.

Reading and heeding God's Word gives us insight for living. So many people today are distressed or despondent because they lack direction and purpose. Most seek answers from the wrong sources. God's Word can be a lamp to our path.

I was once asked to try a simple test. You might like to try it too. You will need a pen and paper. Are you ready? Close your eyes and draw a circle on your page. With your eyes still shut, draw a square around the circle. Without peeping try to draw a triangle inside the circle so that its corners touch the edge of the circle. It is time to open your eyes and

---

[61] John 6:63 (NKJV)

admire your handiwork. If it resembles my attempt, it is not very good. The moral of the exercise is that certain things which are impossible to do in the dark become simple in the light. Likewise, when the light of God's truth shines in our hearts, He shows us how to deal with difficult issues we face. He gives us insight for living. Let's experience God's Word in a fresh new way.

3

Tell Peter

"But go, tell his disciples and Peter, 'He is going ahead of you into Galilee. There you will see him, just as he told you.'"

Mark 16:7 (NIV)

When we look back over our lives, many of us will see a life peppered with both success and failure. Perhaps even now you find yourself facing some failure in your life. The life of Peter, Jesus' friend and disciple, is a lesson for all who are discouraged. Mark's record of the resurrection inserts two short words that offer hope to all who have failed God: "and Peter". The angel at the empty tomb tells the women, "But go, tell His disciples *and Peter...*" Why did the angel add those two words? I am sure that the risen Lord told him specifically to do so.

Peter was at the lowest ebb of his life, but Jesus wanted him to know that he was not forsaken, but forgiven, and that he had a future of service ahead. He is mentioned by name. In other words, the angel said, *"Tell Peter too!"* Why did God single out Peter in this instance? Let's go back to the previous Thursday evening. On that night Peter had denied Jesus three times. This was something Jesus had warned Peter about as they were leaving the upper room for Gethsemane. Peter expressed confidently that this would never happen; he was ready even to die for the Lord. But deny Jesus Peter did – three times. After Jesus was arrested, Peter followed at a distance to the courtyard of Caiaphas' palace. There he was confronted three different times with the accusation that he had been with Jesus, that he was a follower of Jesus. And three times he denied it. With an oath he even confirmed that he never knew Jesus. After the third denial, Jesus passed by, a cock crew and Peter ran out into the night with bitter tears. He had denied his Master.

Now Jesus was risen. And through the angel, Jesus had made special mention of Peter. This could mean only one thing: Jesus was assuring

Peter that He still loved him and counted him as one of His disciples. He still cared for him. Peter was soon to preach his finest sermon:

"Men of Israel, listen to these words: Jesus the Nazarene, a man attested to you by God with miracles and wonders and signs which God performed through Him in your midst, just as you yourselves know – this Man, delivered over by the predetermined plan and foreknowledge of God, you nailed to a cross by the hands of godless men and put Him to death. But God raised Him up again, putting an end to the agony of death, since it was impossible for Him to be held in its power."

Acts 2:22-24 (NASB)

Do you feel discouraged? Are you, like Peter, dismayed at the extent of your inadequacies and the pressure of living by faith? Take heart. God's love is always greater than our failures. The Lord says:

Fear not, for I have redeemed you; I have called you by name, you are mine.

Isaiah 43:1-4 (ESVUK)

4

Steadfast – Immovable – Abounding

Therefore, my beloved brethren, be steadfast, immovable, always abounding in the work of the Lord, knowing that your toil is not in vain in the Lord.

1 Corinthians 15:58 (NASB)

Do you ever get tired or discouraged? Do you ever feel overwhelmed and wonder what's the point? The enemy may be telling you that what you are doing is useless. He may be saying, "Why continue? You might as well quit and do something else." If so, 1 Corinthians 15:58 is just for you.

What does it mean to be "steadfast", "immovable" and "always abounding"?

Steadfast. The Greek word translated "steadfast" means 'seated'. Vine writes that it literally means '*firmly* seated' but implies a fixed purpose of heart.

You will keep in perfect peace
  those whose minds are steadfast,
  because they trust in you.
Trust in the LORD forever,
  for the LORD, the LORD himself, is the Rock eternal.

Isaiah 26:3-4 (NIVUK)

To be steadfast is to be spiritually grounded. A steadfast person knows what he believes and cannot be "tossed back and forth by the waves, and blown here and there by every wind of teaching"[62]. We are to "hold fast the confession of our hope without wavering"[63].

Immoveable. A.W. Pink says that "immovable" is a word implying testing and opposition. Seek grace to say of all troubles and afflictions

---

[62] Ephesians 4:14 (NIV)
[63] Hebrews 10:23 (ESV)

what Paul said of bonds and imprisonments: "None of these things move me."

And now, behold, I go bound in the spirit unto Jerusalem, not knowing the things that shall befall me there. But none of these things move me.

Acts 20:22-24 (KJV)

Abounding. "Abounding" is a translation of the Greek word *perissos* which means 'to exceed the requirements, to superabound, to overflow, to be in affluence, to excel or to be in abundance'. It carries with it the idea of going beyond that which is ordinary.

The motivation for us is surely to remember that it is the work of the Lord: it is His work, His honour and His glory. A further motivation is to remind ourselves that our "toil is not in vain in the Lord". I am thankful that whatever we do for the glory of God does not go unnoticed.

5

Exemplary Living

Let no one look down on your youthfulness, but rather in speech, conduct, love, faith and purity, show yourself an example of those who believe.

1 Timothy 4:12 (NASB)

*P*uritan Thomas Brooks said, "Example is the most powerful rhetoric..." Paul tells us to set an example in 1 Timothy 4:12. *Tupos* is the Greek word for 'example' and it literally means an imprint or impression. The word is used in John 20:25 in reference to the scars upon the hands of Jesus from His Cross. Thomas said:

"Unless I see in His hands the imprint of the nails, and put my finger into the place of the nails, and put my hand into His side, I will not believe."

John 20:25 (NASB)

God has called us to set a thorough example and make an impact with every area of our lives. Paul mentions five ways in which we can set an example for others: speech; conduct; love; faith; purity.

Set an example in speech. What we say matters. This involves our choice of words, the content of our words and the delivery of our words. According to researchers, on an average day we open our mouths 700 times, using about 18,000 words. Does our speech reflect our relationship with Christ? What are the general sorts of words that come out of our mouths daily? Do they build others up or tear them down? Do they encourage others or cast a generally negative light on things? Are they words marked by gratitude because of all Christ has done for us or do we grumble?

Set an example in conduct. Our lifestyle must be worthy of the gospel and calling we have received. How do we treat others? How we react when we are wronged? When others observe our behaviour, can they conclude that we are people of integrity?

Set an example in love. This type of love is sacrificial and unconditional. Do we show a love for God and our neighbour? Do others see love demonstrated in our lives? Others will know we are Christians by the way we love each other. Peter says:

...love one another deeply, from the heart.

1 Peter 1:22 (NIVUK)

Set an example in faith. We need to "hold fast the profession of our faith"[64]. We need to allow our unwavering faith in God and in His Word to be seen by all. Do our lives exhibit faith in Christ? Are they marked by faith and confidence in God? Are we "full of faith"[65]?

Set an example in purity. Jesus tells us in the Sermon on the Mount[66] that the pure in heart shall see God. We need to be diligent in guarding our purity.

How can a young man keep his way pure?
By living according to your word.

Psalm 119:9-11 (WEB)

We can live on a higher level, not according to the world but according to the Word. Are we living on a higher level? Are our motives and intentions pure?

We need to rise up as examples and be the light in the darkest places.

---

[64] Hebrews 10:23
[65] Acts 6:5 (ESV)
[66] See Matthew 5:8

6

Every Day with its New Reasons I will Bless You

[A Psalm] of praise. Of David. I will extol You, my God, O King; and I will bless Your name forever and ever [with grateful, affectionate praise]. Every day [with its new reasons] will I bless You [affectionately and gratefully praise You]; yes, I will praise Your name forever and ever. Great is the Lord and highly to be praised; and His greatness is [so vast and deep as to be] unsearchable.

Psalm 145:1-3 (AMPC)

Notice the title of the Psalm: "[A Psalm] of praise. Of David." The Hebrew superscription of this psalm reads, "*Tehillah* of David." *Tehillah* is a spontaneous new song. It is singing from a melody in your heart by adding words to it. It refers to hymns of the Spirit. The word is found 57 times in the Old Testament. One such example is Psalm 34:1:

...his praise [tehillah] shall continually be in my mouth.

Psalm 34:1 (KJV)

David did not compartmentalise his life into the secular and the sacred. Every day was an opportunity to praise God. His songs did not solely arise when everything was going his way. In fact, it was usually when he was up against things and had relied on God's deliverance that a new song came forth. Take for example, Psalm 40:

I waited patiently for the Lord;
And He inclined to me and heard my cry.
He brought me up out of the pit of destruction, out of the miry clay,
And He set my feet upon a rock making my footsteps firm.
He put a new song in my mouth, a song of praise to our God...

Psalm 40:1-3 (ESV)

We can be like David and determine in our hearts, "Every day [with its new reasons] will I bless You..."

7

Give Me ... Make Me

"The younger of them said to his father, 'Father, give me the share of the estate that falls to me.' ... 'I will get up and go to my father, and will say to him, "Father, I have sinned against heaven, and in your sight; I am no longer worthy to be called your son; make me as one of your hired men."'"

Luke 15:12,18-19 (NASB)

*L*uke 15 resembles God's lost and found department; firstly a story of the lost sheep, then the lost silver coin and finally the lost son. In the parable of the lost son I want you to see something very interesting. Notice the words of the prodigal son "give me!" and then later when he comes to his senses, he says "make me". What a change! He left home saying, "Give me!" He returned home saying, "Make me!"

The younger son went to his father demanding, "Father give me my inheritance." The Living Bible phrases it:

"I want my share of your estate now."

Luke 15:12 (TLB)

Our culture is one of entitlement and grabbing. Cultural forces teach us to claim for all that we can, demand our rights and insist on getting all we are due. Unfortunately, this attitude of heart is not only found in the world. It has slithered its way into the church. "Give me" is such a self-absorbed and indulgent way of looking at things. It is all about me, mine, what I can get and how I can get it. Instead of seeking the Father's heart, too many are solely seeking His hand. Paul tells Timothy about the last days:

People will be lovers of themselves, lovers of money, boastful, proud, abusive, disobedient to their parents, ungrateful.

2 Timothy 3:2 (NIV)

This is the "give me" mentality.

Thankfully the story has not ended. Eventually, as Luke tells us, the son came to his senses. He realised that everything he wanted – and ever needed – was to be found only in the father's house. The key to maturity is "make me", not "give me." *Make me*, Father, what you want me to be. In the beautiful old hymn *Have Thine own way, Lord*, the lyrics of the first stanza read:

> *Have thine own way, Lord! Have thine own way!*
> *Thou art the potter, I am the clay.*
> *Mould me and make me after thy will,*
> *While I am waiting, yielded and still.*

"Give me" brought misery. "Make me" brought joy. What is our mentality today? "Give me" or "make me"?

8

What Shall We Do?

When the servant of the man of God got up and went out early the next morning, an army with horses and chariots had surrounded the city. "Oh no, my lord! What shall we do?" the servant asked. "Don't be afraid," the prophet answered. "Those who are with us are more than those who are with them." And Elisha prayed, "Open his eyes, Lord, so that he may see." Then the Lord opened the servant's eyes, and he looked and saw the hills full of horses and chariots of fire all around Elisha.

2 Kings 6:15-17 (NIV)

What shall we do? This is a question most of us have asked, or will ask, at some point in our lives. The same question was asked in today's reading. Elisha remained calm, relaxed and confident, not in himself, of course, but in His God. In verses 16-17 we learn about how Elisha dealt with his servant's panic. We can connect with the Scripture by applying it to our lives or to help others dealing with the adverse circumstances of life.

Elisha responds by offering a word of encouragement: "Don't be afraid." His servant had allowed fear to grip his heart. He had already witnessed a menu of miracles performed by God through the hand of Elisha, yet still he was afraid because he was processing the events through the eyes on his head and not the eyes of faith. Elisha responds by helping his servant get the correct focus: "...for those who are with us are more than those who are with them." God's innumerable angels allying with Elisha and his servant outnumber the enemy. Elisha responds by prayer for the servant's illumination. The servant was focused on the visible when he needed to see the invisible. God opened the eyes of the servant to see the spiritual reality: the hills were full of fiery holy angels ready to protect Elisha.

Perhaps, like Elisha's servant, we only see the problems. We feel alone. We cry out in despair, "What shall we do?" I know how easy it is to be overwhelmed by fear and worry when faced with difficult situations, but we need to remember that, like Elisha's servant, we don't see the whole picture. We can become so focused on the issue at hand that we lose sight of the fact that we are surrounded by the favour of God, by the grace of God and that God is at work in the midst of our situation. The Psalmist of Psalm 27 knew this well.

> *The LORD is my light and my salvation;*
> *Whom shall I fear?*
> *The LORD is the defence of my life;*
> *Whom shall I dread?*
> *When evildoers came upon me to devour my flesh,*
> *My adversaries and my enemies, they stumbled and fell.*
> *Though a host encamp against me,*
> *My heart will not fear;*
> *Though war arise against me,*
> *In spite of this I shall be confident.*
>
> *Psalm 27:1-3 (NKJV)*

Remember this: the Lord outnumbers any of the dangers surrounding you, all of the fears within you and whatever makes you worry. The church is not in defeat and it should not be in retreat. Our God is greater. Our God is stronger.

9

Is There Anyone to Whom I May Show the Kindness of God?

The king said, "Is there not yet anyone of the house of Saul to whom I may show the kindness of God?"

2 Samuel 9:3 (NASB)

This was a question which totally transformed a man's life. The man was Mephibosheth. The person asking the question was King David. David had been crowned king of Israel. It was common practice in those days to exterminate all members of a previous dynasty to prevent any descendant from seeking the throne. As long as a spark of life from that family still smouldered, it was a threat to the new king. Yet David's response, as we have just read, was quite the contrary. In fact, David's actions draw us to reflect upon the theme of kindness in our lives. This biblical story practically illustrates the kindness and grace of God extended to us. Mephibosheth deserved nothing and yet David favoured him. He was crippled as the result of a fall and yet David lifted him up and seated him at his table. God's kindness brings us into a place of intimate communion with God.

The first section of Proverbs 19:22 states:

What is desired in a man is kindness...

Proverbs 19:22 (NKJV)

Why? Why would God consider this trait so important? The truth is that we are the vessels today to extend God's lovingkindness and mercy to the world around us. Kindness is humbly giving of ourselves in love and mercy to others who may not be able to give anything back, who sometimes don't deserve it and who frequently don't thank us for it. Kindness is not an inconvenience to be avoided, but a characteristic to be embraced. Sometimes it is as simple as a pleasant smile, or a warm handshake, or sending a thank you note, or assisting a neighbour with a household chore, or being with a friend in distress.

> *And be kind to one another, tenderhearted, forgiving one another, even as God in Christ forgave you.*
>
> *Ephesians 4:32 (NKJV)*

Kindness is indeed the amazing quality of being friendly, generous and considerate. It is to flow out of our being as genuine affection, appreciation, warmth, understanding, unselfishness and thoughtfulness. David's words offer a model prayer for all of us at the start of each new day: *is there anyone to whom I can show God's kindness today?*

10

By My God I Can

For by You I can run upon a troop;
And by my God I can leap over a wall.

Psalm 18:29 (NASB)

Time and again God has demonstrated His power in the midst of His people. Throughout their history, He has proven that He is stronger than every obstacle they ever faced. Today's verse is all about running through troops and leaping over walls!

In today's verse we see the words "by You". *By my God.* Psalm 18 is a song of triumph in which David ascribes his victories to God. He exalts and magnifies Him throughout it and shows us how reliant he is on Him. For example:

The LORD is my rock and my fortress and my deliverer, my God, my rock, in whom I take refuge...

Psalm 18:2 (ESVUK)

I call upon the LORD, who is worthy to be praised, and I am saved from my enemies.

Psalm 18:3 (ESVUK)

...my cry for help came before Him, into His very ears.

Psalm 18:6 (AMP)

For You have girded me with strength for battle;
You have subdued under me those who rose up against me.

Psalm 18:39 (NKJV)

What is the wall before you that is posing insurmountable today? You can call upon God for help. Look to the One who is Your rock and fortress and deliverer. Allow your cries to come before Him, into his very ears. He will gird you with strength for battle so that you too can testify, "For by You I can run upon a troop; And by my God I can leap over a wall." This is Paul's assertion in Philippians 4:13:

I can do all things through Him who strengthens me.

Philippians 4:13 (ESVUK)

The key words are "through Him". *He* is the One who strengthens us, or, as the Greek suggests, He is the One who 'pours strength into us'. He is the One who enables us to say, "I can." 'Can' is a positive word. It focuses on what is possible, not impossible.

"...with God all things are possible."

Matthew 19:26 (NKJV)

I encourage you this week to look to Him and start believing, "By You I can... By my God I can... I can do all things through Him who strengthens me."

11

Request and Rest

Be careful for nothing; but in every thing by prayer and supplication with thanksgiving let your requests be made known unto God. And the peace of God, which passeth all understanding, shall keep your hearts and minds through Christ Jesus.

Philippians 4:6-7 (KJV)

Don't worry about anything; instead, pray about everything; tell God your needs, and don't forget to thank him for his answers. If you do this, you will experience God's peace, which is far more wonderful than the human mind can understand. His peace will keep your thoughts and your hearts quiet and at rest as you trust in Christ Jesus.

Philippians 4:6-7 (TLB)

When faced with a challenge or crisis, our tendency is sometimes to get all anxious about it. But God does not want us to react this way. He does not want us to be anxious about anything. He wants us to go to Him in prayer and supplication, telling Him what we need and thanking Him for the answer. He wants us to *request* and then *rest* in the assurance that He is able to answer.

Entertain no anxious cares, but throw them all upon God.

Philippians 4:6-7 (Lightfoot)

The word 'cares' refers to a troubled state of mind resulting from concern about current or potential difficulties. It comes from an Old English word that means 'to strangle' and paints the picture of being pulled in different directions. "Be careful for nothing." In the original Greek sentence Paul places the word "nothing" at the beginning for emphasis. "Nothing" literally means 'not even one thing'. Peter offered similar advice writing:

Humble yourselves, therefore, under God's mighty hand, that he may lift you up in due time. Cast all your anxiety on him because he cares for you.

1 Peter 5:6-7 (NIV)

The word for "requests" in today's passage refers to detailed prayer about specific issues. We need to learn to pray specifically and not in generalities. We should never be afraid to approach God with the specific needs of life. Cultivate the habit of referring all things, great or small, to God in prayer. Is it not breathtaking to hear Jesus say, "Ask, and it will be given to you; seek, and you will find; knock, and it will be opened to you."[67]? Is it not reassuring to hear Him say, "Come unto Me, all ye that labour and are heavy-laden, and I will give you rest ... and ye shall find rest unto your souls"[68]?

So *request* and *rest* today.

---

[67] Matthew 7:7 (ESVUK)
[68] Matthew 11:28-29 (KJV)

12

Such as I Have

Now Peter and John went up together into the temple at the hour of prayer, being the ninth hour. And a certain man lame from his mother's womb was carried, whom they laid daily at the gate of the temple which is called Beautiful, to ask alms of them that entered into the temple; who seeing Peter and John about to go into the temple asked an alms. And Peter, fastening his eyes upon him with John, said, Look on us. And he gave heed unto them, expecting to receive something of them. Then Peter said, Silver and gold have I none; but such as I have give I thee: in the name of Jesus Christ of Nazareth rise up and walk.

Acts 3:1-6 (KJV)

Chuck Swindoll remarked, "We are all faced with a series of great opportunities brilliantly disguised as impossible situations." In Acts 2 Luke has described the early church by saying:

Everyone was filled with awe, and many wonders and miraculous signs were done by the apostles.

Acts 2:43 (NIVUK)

In Acts 3 we see an 'impossible situation' miraculously transformed and the purpose of Pentecost lived out in the lives of Peter and John.

Notice the phrase "such as I have give I thee" in today's passage. This phrase can also be translated, "But what I've been given, what I have been filled with, I give to you."

This was just an ordinary day in the life of Peter and John. It was 3pm in the afternoon.[69] For this crippled man, it was also an ordinary day; in fact, every day was the same: the same spot, the same crowd, the same scene, the same routine. The congregation going to prayer "recognized

---

[69] It was the ninth hour, in the reckoning of the Jewish clock – 3 o'clock in the afternoon.

him as the same man who used to sit begging at the temple gate called Beautiful, and they were filled with wonder and amazement at what had happened to him."[70].

Imagine how many people simply ignored this beggar each day. Think of how many people we encounter on a daily basis who are going through difficulty and are just hoping someone will notice and offer to help. For this man, the day would be different because he was about to encounter God and experience a total change in his life. Why? Because Peter and John would be walking by soon and were willing to be channels of God's love. Do you know what it means to become a channel of God's love? It means God is simply using you as an instrument with which He can serve His purpose. I believe there are many divine appointments and opportunities in our lives if only we would be willing to be channel of blessing to others and say, "Such as I have give I thee."

---

[70] Acts 3:10 (NIV)

13

They Strengthened Their Hands

Then I told them of the hand of my God which was good upon me; as also the king's words that he had spoken unto me. And they said, Let us rise up and build. So they strengthened their hands for this good work.

Nehemiah 2:18 (KJV)

*T*hey strengthened their hands. Before anything great can be accomplished and the vision reinforced, we must understand the reason and purpose for being on the wall. Nehemiah made the purpose clear and the people united for the task.

Paul said:

But whatever happens to me, remember always to live as Christians should, so that whether I ever see you again or not, I will keep on hearing good reports that you are standing side by side with one strong purpose – to tell the Good News.

Philippians 1:27 (TLB)

Are we standing side by side with one strong purpose? Have we resolved to "rise up and build"? Are we strengthening our hands for this good work? As the Message Bible puts it:

They said, "We're with you. Let's get started." They rolled up their sleeves, ready for the good work.

Nehemiah 2:18 (MSG)

In Exodus 17 we read of a momentous occasion in Israel's history. Moses was unable to hold his hands up, and if they fell then the Amalekites would certainly win the battle. However, Aaron and Hur stepped forth and held the hands of Moses up until the battle was won. It is a beautiful picture of partnership and working together with one purpose.

So "they strengthened their hands" in Nehemiah. Nehemiah put different people working on different places of the wall. Not everyone did the same thing, but they were working toward the same goal. Keep reading through the book. In chapter 6 the enemy continued to oppose their plans. Nehemiah said:

> *They were all trying to frighten us, thinking, "Their hands will get too weak for the work, and it will not be completed." But I prayed, "Now strengthen my hands."*
>
> Nehemiah 6:9 (NIV)

God answers Nehemiah's prayer and the rebuilding project continues. Under Nehemiah's leadership, the walls are rebuilt in fifty-two days. May God strengthen your hands now. May you fulfil your assignment.

14

Love is in the Air

Because Thy lovingkindness is better than life,
My lips will praise Thee.

Psalm 63:3 (KJV)

*V*alentine's Day traditions date back to the 5th century, and whether you love it or loathe it, it's still going strong today and is a very lucrative time for card shops. Rummaging in the attic one day I stumbled upon an old box which contained a very bright pink Valentine's card sent to me from my husband (then boyfriend). It was covered in xoxoxoxoxo – I mean, thousands of them, all around the edges and in between!

Have you even wondered about how an 'X' got to symbolise a kiss and an 'O' a hug? There are many theories proposed but there is a general agreement that it can be traced back to a time when few people could write and in place of their signature they would sign important documents with an 'X', to show that what they had written was true. 'X' was also a Christian symbol resembling the cross where Jesus was crucified and very similar to the Greek letter *chi*, which is the first letter in the word 'Christ'. It thus symbolised credibility and trust. There is a lack of definitiveness about the history of 'O' but it does look like an embrace, doesn't it?

As we think of love today, I challenge you to reflect on the Source of all love. In the Old Testament we find a word called *hesed* which is one of the richest, most powerful words. It is difficult to translate. No single word in English captures its meaning. Translators use words such as "kindness" and "loyal love". We saw it in today's verse, in the word "lovingkindness".

In Psalm 136 the central message of the entire psalm is the truth that God's lovingkindness or steadfast love (*hesed*) endures forever. *Hesed* is mentioned in every one of the twenty-six verses in Psalm 136. I love how it is translated in *The Jesus Storybook Bible:*

Never-Stopping, Never-Giving-Up, Unbreaking, Always and Forever Love.

God loves you with a never stopping, never giving up, unbreaking, always and forever love. It is a love which is immeasurable, steadfast and permanent. God says:

My love for you is forever.

Psalm 136:1 (GNT)

Nothing can stop me from loving you.

Romans 8:38-39 (GNT)

My love for you is greater than you can ever imagine.

Ephesians 3:17-18 (GNT)

Happy Valentine's Day!

15

Enter with the Password "Thank You"

Enter into his gates with thanksgiving, and into his courts with praise: be thankful unto him, and bless his name.
For the LORD is good; his mercy is everlasting; and his truth endures to all generations.

Psalm 100:4-5 (KJV)

For anyone who is a regular web user, remembering passwords is a complicated business. Surely I'm not the only one scratching my head and trying to recall the unique uppercase and lowercase letter-number-and-symbol codes I once created to access my various online accounts? LinkedIn, Skype, Facebook, Twitter, bank accounts, Apple ID, Instagram, YouTube, Vimeo, eBay, PayPal, Yahoo to name a few! Forgotten your password? Yes! The Urban Dictionary now includes the term which the internet has coined 'passworditis' – forgetting a password.

The psalmist gives us a useful password in Psalm 100:4

Enter with the password: "Thank you!" Make yourselves at home, talking praise. Thank Him. Worship Him. For God is sheer beauty, all-generous in love, loyal always and ever.

Psalm 100:4-5 (MSG)

The password "thank you" is easy to remember, but too often forgotten when it comes to worship. It's important to be reminded of this password. Paul says:

...give thanks in all circumstances, for this is God's will for you in Christ Jesus.

1 Thessalonians 5:18 (NIV)

In another scripture he says:

...always giving thanks to God the Father for everything in the name of our Lord Jesus Christ.

Ephesians 5:20 (NIV)

Do you remember the ten lepers in Luke's Gospel? Jesus, on his way to Jerusalem, was going through the region between Samaria and Galilee, and as He entered a village, he came upon a leper colony. Ten of them sought healing but nine of them forgot the password "thank you". Only one remembered.

And one of them, when he saw that he was healed, turned back, and with a loud voice glorified God, and fell down on his face at his feet, giving him thanks: and he was a Samaritan.

Luke 17:15-16 (NKJV)

Let us not become complacent in our thanksgiving. There is a danger in having plenty; when all our needs are met – food, shelter, clothing – we tend to settle back and enjoy the extra things with which God has blessed us. If we forget the source of our wealth, or even worse, we pat ourselves on the back and take the credit for our wealth, then we have forgotten and ignored God, the source of all provision.

Let us not forget to say thank you to God.

16

Through

When you pass through the waters, I will be with you;
And through the rivers, they will not overflow you.
When you walk through the fire, you will not be scorched,
Nor will the flame burn you.

Isaiah 43:2 (NASB, emphasis added)

*E*veryone faces challenges and hardships at different points in their lives, but the important thing is to continue to trust God in the midst of those storms. In Isaiah 43:2 notice the words "when" and "through". It shows us that difficulties are inevitable but they are temporary and we need the mindset that we are going through them and out the other side. "Through" is actually one of God's favourite words. No matter how 'rough and tough' things may be, God is bringing you *through*.

Even though I walk through the valley of the shadow of death,
I fear no evil, for You are with me;
Your rod and Your staff, they comfort me.

Psalm 23:4 (NASB, emphasis added)

Passing through the Valley of Weeping (Baca), they make it a place of springs; the early rain also covers it with blessings.

Psalm 84:6 (AMP, emphasis added)

I noticed in the news that one of the world's longest and deepest rail tunnels has officially opened in Switzerland and apparently is 35 miles long. That's quite a distance to be in a tunnel and sometimes in life our troubles make us feel like we are in an endless tunnel. It's never easy or enjoyable in the tunnel, but it's only temporary. As Corrie Ten Boom once put it:

When the train goes through a tunnel and it gets dark, you don't throw away the ticket and jump off. You sit still and trust the engineer.

Remember, it is God who brings us *through*.

17

Selah

I will abide in thy tabernacle for ever: I will trust in the covert of thy wings. Selah.

Psalm 61:4 (KJV)

*H*ave you noticed that the word *selah* appears often when reading the Psalms?

Trust in him at all times; ye people, pour out your heart before him: God is a refuge for us. Selah.

Psalm 62:8 (KJV)

All the earth shall worship thee, and shall sing unto thee; they shall sing to thy name. Selah.

Psalms 66:4 (KJV)

Blessed be the Lord, who daily loadeth us with benefits, even the God of our salvation. Selah.

Psalms 68:19 (KJV)

Blessed are they that dwell in thy house: they will be still praising thee. Selah.

Psalms 84:4 (KJV)

What does *selah* mean? We are probably familiar with the two Hebrew words *amen* and *hallelujah*, but did you know that *selah* is used three times as often in the Old Testament as those words? In fact, *selah* is used in over a quarter of the psalms.

Why is it there? Apparently, it is considered a technical musical term for an instrumental interlude because the psalms were often set to music. To refer to the dictionary of Hebrew terms, *selah* is a Hebrew word meaning "a musical interlude; to pause and think about what was just said or sung; or to pause and watch for a visual demonstration of what was said or sung". The Amplified Bible adds "pause, and calmly think about that" to each verse where *selah* appears. Thus today's verse reads:

I will dwell in Your tabernacle forever; let me find refuge and trust in the shelter of Your wings. Selah [pause, and calmly think of that]!

Psalm 61:4 (AMPC)

It's more than a word; it's an instruction. *Selah* asks us to stop, pause, and think about the ramifications of what we have read.

Commentaries offer two other viable meanings based on Hebrew root word study: 'to be weighed'; 'to exalt'. We should pause to carefully weigh the meaning of what we have just read or heard, and we should exalt or lift the name of the Lord.

It reminds me of a little saying I heard years ago: "If we pause to think, we have cause to thank." Ponder the deep implications of what has been written and thank God for His work in your life.

18

But We...

Some trust in chariots and some in horses, but we trust in the name of the LORD our God.

Psalm 20:7 (ESVUK)

his verse is taken from the end of Psalm 20 and it comes with a challenge; it is packed with a punch: *where is your trust and confidence?* Do you misplace your trust in human power or place your trust in heavenly provision? The challenge is to live on a different level. Notice the words, "Some ... and some ... but we..." Many place their trust in the wrong things.

Jeremiah writes:

This is what the LORD says: "Cursed is the one who trusts in man, who draws strength from mere flesh and whose heart turns away from the LORD. ... But blessed is the one who trusts in the LORD, whose confidence is in Him."

Jeremiah 17:5,7 (NIV)

Notice that a person who puts their trust in God is described as "blessed". We are also told in the same chapter that this person does not fear when heat comes and has no worries in a year of drought.

O LORD of hosts,
Blessed is the man who trusts in You!

Psalm 84:12 (NKJV)

To trust in the name of the Lord our God means to trust in the revealed character of God. We trust His wisdom. We trust that His way is perfect. We trust that He does not fail us or forsake us. We trust that His name is a strong tower.

And those who know Your name will put their trust in You;
For You, LORD, have not forsaken those who seek You.

Psalm 9:10 (NKJV)

When David fought Goliath, he did not really depend on his sling shot and those five smooth stones. He was glad he had them, but his total confidence was in God. He knew that neither Goliath's weapons nor Goliath's size would give Goliath victory because David was the one that came to that battle in the name of God.

Then said David to the Philistine, Thou comest to me with a sword, and with a spear, and with a shield: but I come to thee in the name of the LORD of hosts, the God of the armies of Israel, whom thou hast defied.

1 Samuel 17:45 (KJV)

As we confront the Goliath battles that appear in our personal lives and that face our nations, we need to direct our focus away from what mankind is doing and look instead at what God is doing.

It is better to take refuge in the LORD than to trust in man.

Psalm 118:8 (AMP)

In the Message Bible, Psalm 20:7-8 reads:

See those people polishing their chariots,
    and those others grooming their horses?
    But we're making garlands for GOD our God. T
he chariots will rust,
    those horses pull up lame –
    and we'll be on our feet, standing tall.

Psalm 20:7-8 (MSG)

I encourage you to...

Trust in the LORD, and do good;
Dwell in the land, and feed on His faithfulness.
Delight yourself also in the LORD,
And He shall give you the desires of your heart.
Commit your way to the LORD,

February

Trust also in Him,
And He shall bring it to pass.

Psalm 37:3-5 (NKJV)

19

Did Someone Whisper?

My sheep hear My voice, and I know them, and they follow Me.
John 10:27 (NKJV)

*M*any radio and television stations transmit twenty-four hours a day, seven days a week; but we only hear them when we turn the receiver on and tune it in. Failure to hear the signal does not mean that the station is not transmitting. Likewise, God is constantly transmitting His voice to His sheep, but few are tuned in.

The prophet Elijah had an awesome encounter with God, and it happened at the lowest moment in his life. The story, in 1 Kings 19, begins with the prophet hiding in a cave.

"Elijah, why are you here?" the Lord asked.

Exhausted, Elijah explained, "I have zealously served the Lord God Almighty. But the people of Israel have broken their covenant with you, torn down your altars, and killed every one of your prophets. I am the only one left, and now they are trying to kill me, too."[71]

Elijah was ready to call it quits. But the Lord asked him to do something. He said, "Go out and stand on the mountain. I want you to see me when I pass by."

Elijah obeyed. But before he could step out of the cave, a mighty windstorm hit the mountainside. But the Lord was not in the wind, or the violent earthquake that followed. He wasn't in the fire that rained from heaven after that. Instead, "there was the sound of a gentle whisper"[72]. Elijah knew it was the Lord. He got up, wrapped his face in his cloak and went out and stood at the entrance of the cave.

The gentle voice asked Elijah the same question as before: "Elijah, why are you here?"

Elijah repeated his earlier answer.

---

[71] 1 Kings 19:14 (NLT)
[72] 1 Kings 19:12 (NLT)

Then, the Lord gave Elijah further instructions for ministry and assured him he wasn't on his own.

To hear someone's whisper, you need to be near. Whispering does not work very well if you're speaking to someone who's standing on the other side of the room. God doesn't want a long-distance relationship; He wants a close, intimate one. Jesus said:

> *"…he goes before them; and the sheep follow him, for they know his voice. … My sheep hear My voice, and I know them, and they follow Me."*
>
> *John 10:4,27 (NKJV)*

Learning to clearly distinguish God's voice is invaluable. Jesus said regarding His sheep that they will not follow the voice of the stranger.

> *Yet they will by no means follow a stranger, but will flee from him, for they do not know the voice of strangers.*
>
> *John 10:5 (NKJV)*

Whose voice are you following? Are you tuned in to God's voice?

> *Listen for GOD's voice in everything you do, everywhere you go; he's the one who will keep you on track.*
>
> *Proverbs 3:6 (MSG)*

Jesus says in Revelation 3:20:

> *Behold, I stand at the door and knock. If anyone hears my voice and opens the door, I will come in to him and eat with him, and he with me.*
>
> *Revelation 3:20 (ESVUK)*

Isaiah states:

> *Your ears shall hear a word behind you, saying,*
> *"This is the way, walk in it,"*
> *Whenever you turn to the right hand*
> *Or whenever you turn to the left.*
>
> *Isaiah 30:21 (NKJV)*

20

Do It God's Way

He [Jesus] said to Simon, "Put out into the deep water and let down your nets for a catch." Simon answered and said, "Master, we worked hard all night and caught nothing, but I will do as You say and let down the nets." When they had done this, they enclosed a great quantity of fish, and their nets began to break; so they signalled to their partners in the other boat for them to come and help them. And they came and filled both of the boats, so that they began to sink.

Luke 5:4-7 (NASB)

rank Sinatra sang the words, "I did it my way," and many people have lived out that sentiment. Take, for example, the episode with the new cart in 2 Samuel 6. David's desire was clear and simple. He wanted the Ark returned to its place as the centrepiece of worship and devotion in Israel. He wanted God placed back in the centre of the national consciousness. His motive was pure but his method was wrong. The construction and transportation of the Ark was clearly communicated through Moses to the people in the Scriptures. It was to be carried with staves of wood through the rings on the side of the Ark,[73] and transported only by the Levites.[74] David, however, did it his way and transported it on a new cart. The Bible says that they "set the Ark of God upon a new cart"[75]. David made good plans and good preparations, but he neglected to do it God's way. He paid a high price for this decision. In Proverbs 14:12 we read:

There is a way which seems right to a man, but in the end it leads to death.

Proverbs 14:12 (WEB)

---

[73] See Exodus 25:15,28
[74] See Numbers 1:50
[75] 2 Samuel 6:3 (KJV)

Let's take another example, Saul, in 1 Samuel 15. God told him:

Now go and smite Amalek, and utterly destroy all that they have; do not spare them, but kill both man and woman, infant and suckling, ox and sheep, camel and ass.

1 Samuel 15:3 (KJV)

Did Saul do that? Verse 9 describes his fatal disobedience.

But Saul and the people spared Agag, and the best of the sheep and of the oxen and of the fatlings, and the lambs, and of all that was good, and would not utterly destroy them; all that was despised and worthless they utterly destroyed.

1 Samuel 15:9 (KJV)

He spared the best of the cattle and sheep – and he spared King Agag. In other words, he did it his way and again with disastrous results.

Take a further example, Luke 5. Peter and his friends had been out fishing all night, and they were up on the shore cleaning their nets. It had been a rough night – they had worked hard – but they hadn't caught a thing! Jesus said to Simon, "Put out into the deep water and let down your nets for a catch."

There were all kinds of reasons Peter could have given for not doing this: firstly, Jesus wasn't a fisherman; secondly, it was the wrong time of the day for fishing (it was too hot); and besides, Peter and his friends were tired – they had been out all night. But Peter chose to be obedient and we see what happened when he followed the directions from Christ.

When they pulled up their nets, they were shocked to see a huge catch of fish, so much that their nets were ready to burst!

Luke 5:6 (TPT)

God's way is best.

21

As You Go

"As you go, proclaim this message: 'The kingdom of heaven has come near.'"

Matthew 10:7 (NIV)

ecently I heard a statement which made me sit up and take notice. It was this: "Don't become so focused on the destination that you forget to enjoy the journey." That's good advice. So often in life we can be so focused on getting from A to B. Even in our everyday situations we can set ourselves ironclad goals and stringent objectives which leave little room for God's intervention. The danger is that we miss the opportunity to minister 'on the way' and to be open to God's leading 'as we go'. As we read through the Gospels we find that a large proportion of Jesus' ministry was actually *en route* from one place to another. The journey was important.

Matthew 28:19 is translated:

"Therefore, go and make disciples…"

Matthew 28:19 (NLT)

But the original Greek construction of the sentence is, "As you go, make disciples…" Jesus was on the road a lot and many of His ministry opportunities arose in that context. In John 4 we see Jesus traveling from Judea to Galilee through Samaria. As He rested by a well near Sychar, He encountered a Samaritan woman. The end result was that she and many other Samaritans became believers. As He was on the road from Jericho,[76] He ministered to Bartimaeus who received his sight. On the Emmaus road two despondent hearts trudged along and the Bible tells us that…

---

[76] See Mark 10:46-52

...Jesus himself came up and walked along with them.

Luke 24:15 (NIVUK)

It wasn't long before their burdened hearts became burning hearts and their lives were changed forever.

As He went about, what did He do?

"You know of Jesus of Nazareth, how God anointed Him with the Holy Spirit and with power, and how He went about doing good and healing all who were oppressed by the devil, for God was with Him."

Acts 10:38 (NASB)

As He was on His way from one place to another, many were healed, lives were transformed, storms were stilled.

When Gordon MacDonald pastored Trinity Baptist Church in New York City, he would ride the same bus daily from his home to the church. One day the bus driver complained to MacDonald, "You've got it a lot better than me. You have an interesting job and travel different places. I just drive this bus up and down the same streets every day."

MacDonald told the bus driver his job could be a Christian ministry too. "Every day, when you first get on this bus, before anyone else gets on, dedicate the bus to God for that day. Declare it to be a sanctuary for God for that day. Consecrate it to God's glory, and then act like it is a place where God dwells."

Several weeks later MacDonald returned from a trip and saw the bus driver. "You've transformed my life," the man exclaimed. "I've been doing what you said every day, and it has made me see my job in an entirely new perspective."

The same transformation can happen to us if we would adjust our attitude each day and realise life is about what happens as we go.

22

Don't Throw in the Towel

And let us not be weary in well doing: for in due season we shall reap, if we faint not.

Galatians 6:9 (KJV)

"Don't throw in the towel" derives from the world of boxing. When a boxer is suffering a beating and his corner want to stop the fight, they literally throw in the towel to indicate their conceding of the fight. In today's passage the Bible encourages us not to 'throw in the towel'!

Let's take time to read this verse in few translations and allow it to sink in.

So let's not get tired of doing what is good. At just the right time we will reap a harvest of blessing if we don't give up.

Galatians 6:9 (NLT)

Let us not lose heart in doing good, for in due time we will reap if we do not grow weary.

Galatians 6:9 (NASB)

And let us not lose heart and grow weary and faint in acting nobly and doing right, for in due time and at the appointed season we shall reap, if we do not loosen and relax our courage and faint.

Galatians 6:9 (AMP)

And let us not get tired of doing what is right, for after a while we will reap a harvest of blessing if we don't get discouraged and give up.

Galatians 6:9 (TLB)

So let's not allow ourselves to get fatigued doing good. At the right time we will harvest a good crop if we don't give up, or quit.

Galatians 6:9 (MSG)

Growing weary in doing good is an ever-present danger in the Christian life. Paul, perhaps better than anyone else, knew how wearying the spiritual battle can be and the dangers we face. However, at the end of his ministry he was able to declare that he had finished his course.[77] The only way to finish our course is to avoid becoming weary in well-doing. The Greek word for "weary" is *ekkakeo* which means 'to lose heart, to be wearied out, exhausted'. It's the same word Jesus used in Luke 18:1:

> And He spake a parable unto them to this end, that men ought always to pray, and not to faint.
>
> *Luke 18:1 (KJV)*

Ekkakeo can mean to lose our motivation in continuing a particular activity and so to become discouraged and give up, the opposite of being "steadfast, immovable, always abounding in the work of the Lord, knowing that your toil is not in vain in the Lord"[78].

In the words of Hebrews 12 may we be encouraged to...

> ...run with perseverance the race marked out for us, fixing our eyes on Jesus, the pioneer and perfecter of faith. For the joy set before him he endured the cross, scorning its shame, and sat down at the right hand of the throne of God. Consider Him who endured such opposition from sinners, so that you will not grow weary and lose heart.
>
> *Hebrews 12:1-3 (NIVUK)*

---

[77] See 2 Timothy 4:7
[78] 1 Corinthians 15:58 (NASB)

23

Fixing Our Eyes on Jesus

Therefore, since we have so great a cloud of witnesses surrounding us, let us also lay aside every encumbrance and the sin which so easily entangles us, and let us run with endurance the race that is set before us, fixing our eyes on Jesus, the author and perfecter of faith, who for the joy set before Him endured the cross, despising the shame, and has sat down at the right hand of the throne of God.

Hebrews 12:1-2 (NASB)

I want us to zoom in on the words "fixing our eyes on Jesus".

...looking with undivided attention...

Hebrews 12:2 (Analysed Literal)

...looking away [from all that will distract] to Jesus...

Hebrews 12:2 (AMP)

The Greek word is *apharao* which is made up of *apo* ('away from something near') and *horao* ('look, see, behold'). It is good to glance at the cloud of witnesses and be encouraged by their faithful finish, but it is essential that we firmly fix our gaze on our Saviour Jesus.

John Phillips writes that believers should especially look at:

- *His person* – He is the author and perfecter of faith;
- *His passion* – who for the joy set before Him endured the cross;
- *His position* – has sat down at the right hand of the throne of God.

I remember hearing of a farmer who was teaching his son to plough with a mule.

"To make straight furrows, son, just pick out an object beyond the field and keep your eyes fixed on it."

The boy nodded to affirm his understanding and the farmer left.

When he came back an hour later, the farmer was shocked to see a field of twisted furrows. "What happened, son? I thought I told you to keep your eye on an object beyond the field."

"I did, Dad," the boy replied, pointing to the 'standard' he had chosen – a cow in the adjoining pasture!

That humorous story holds a serious lesson for us. Whether we are ploughing a field or running our race, it's critical that we keep our eyes on the right target. Let's fix our eyes on Jesus afresh.

24

No Longer I Who Live, but Christ Lives in Me

I have been crucified with Christ; it is no longer I who live, but Christ lives in me; and the life which I now live in the flesh I live by faith in the Son of God, who loved me and gave Himself for me.

Galatians 2:20 (NKJV)

The Greek Interlinear puts it this way: "And I no longer live but in me Christ lives." As believers we are alive to Jesus Christ and Jesus is alive in us. Why? Because:

He loved me
and
gave Himself for me

What are the lifestyle implications of this truth? Pauls tells us, "I have been crucified with Christ." Or, as he said to the Romans:

...knowing this, that our old man is crucified with him, that the body of sin might be destroyed, that henceforth we should not serve sin.

Romans 6:6 (KJV)

There was a vast difference between 'Saul of Tarsus' and 'Paul the Apostle'. Before his conversion he was a persecutor attempting to destroy the church. Now he lived to spread the gospel of the same Jesus that he once persecuted! He was dead to the old way of living.

Paul also tell us, "I no longer live." Or, as he said in 2 Corinthians 5:15:

He died for all, so that all those who live would no longer live for themselves, but for Him who died and was raised for their sake.

2 Corinthians 5:15 (AMP)

193

Paul also tells us, "Christ lives in me." Realise Who is in you:

Christ in you, the hope of glory...

Colossians 1:27 (KJV)

Then Paul says, "The life which I now live, I live by faith in the Son of God." It is a life of total dependency in Him.

Looking unto Jesus the author and finisher of faith...

Hebrews 12:2 (KJV)

Four times in the Bible we are told, "The righteous shall live by faith."[79] Living by faith will take our life out of the natural and into the supernatural. Faith is standing on God's integrity and acting on His promises.

Can you say what Paul said?

He loved me and gave Himself for me.

I have been crucified with Christ.

I no longer live.

But Christ lives in me.

The life which I now live, I live by faith in the Son of God.

---

[79] Habakkuk 2:4; Romans 1:17; Galatians 3:11; Hebrews 10:38

25

God Adverts

You are the light of the world. A town built on a hill cannot be hidden. Neither do people light a lamp and put it under a bowl. Instead they put it on its stand, and it gives light to everyone in the house. In the same way, let your light shine before others, that they may see your good deeds and glorify your Father in heaven.

Matthew 5:14-16 (NIVUK)

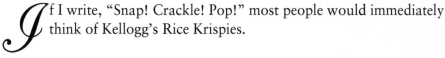 f I write, "Snap! Crackle! Pop!" most people would immediately think of Kellogg's Rice Krispies.

Let's try some more.
1. "Just Do It"
2. "Share moments. Share life"
3. "I'm Lovin' It"
4. "When you care enough to send the very best"
5. "It does exactly what it says on the tin"
6. "Think different"
7. "Have it your way"
8. "Because you're worth it"
9. "Eat fresh"
10. "Taste the rainbow"
11. "They're Gr-r-r-reat"
12. "Every little helps"

Answers:
1. Nike
2. Kodak
3. McDonald's
4. Hallmark
5. Ronseal
6. Apple
7. Burger King
8. L'Oréal
9. Subway
10. Skittles
11. Frosties
12. Tesco

The best advertising slogans are the ones that truly describe what a brand stands for, stick in the consumer's mind and help the product to stand out. Such is the power of advertising. That made me think: what do people think of when they see you and I today? We are God's audio-visual presentation here to billboard His greatness and promote Him in every area of life. Jesus tells us:

You are the light of the world.

Matthew 5:14 (NIVUK)

Jesus did not say, "You are the light of the church." He said, "You are the light of the *world*." Our Christianity should be evident to all. We are here to reflect God. We are here to love others like Jesus. We are here to put God on display to the world. Our good deeds ought to draw attention, not to ourselves, but to God.

May God be glorified in your life today.

26

How Lovely

How lovely are Your dwelling places,
O LORD of hosts!
My soul longed and even yearned for the courts of the LORD;
My heart and my flesh sing for joy to the living God ...
For a day in Your courts is better than a thousand outside.

Psalm 84:1-2,10 (NASB)

This week I noticed two places in the Bible where you find the words "How lovely!" (There may be more, but these were brought to my attention.)
The first is Psalm 84:

How lovely are Your dwelling places, O LORD of hosts!

Psalm 84:1 (NASB)

How lovely it is when we get close to God and seek His face, when simply being in His Presence is our priority. The psalmist says in Psalm 27:4

One thing I have desired of the LORD,
That will I seek:
That I may dwell in the house of the LORD
All the days of my life,
To behold the beauty of the LORD...

Psalm 27:4 (NKJV)

How many of us can say with the Psalmist that the one thing we desire and seek after in life is to dwell in the Presence of God and behold His beauty? James tells us that we have an awesome promise:

Draw near to God and He will draw near to you.

James 4:8 (NASB)

When we take the time to draw near and to be in His presence, we realise how wonderful He is.

O LORD, our Lord,
How majestic is Your name in all the earth!

Psalm 8:9 (NASB)

How great is Your goodness...

Psalm 31:19 (NASB)

How precious is Your lovingkindness, O God!

Psalm 36:7 (NASB)

Say to God, "How awesome are Your works!"

Psalm 66:3 (NASB)

How sweet are Your words to my taste!
Yes, sweeter than honey to my mouth!

Psalm 119:103 (NASB)

How unsearchable are His judgments and unfathomable His ways!

Romans 11:33 (NASB)

How lovely it is to dwell with Him and He with us, as the Psalmist experienced.

The other place where I discovered the words "how lovely" is in Isaiah.

How lovely on the mountains
Are the feet of him who brings good news,
Who announces peace
And brings good news of happiness,
Who announces salvation,
And says to Zion, "Your God reigns!"

Isaiah 52:7 (NASB)

Not only is it lovely to spend time with Him, it is such a lovely privilege to go in His name and share His good news and tell the world that our God reigns. It is a blessing to be able to share God's good news of redemption, salvation and peace with others. With whom do you need to share the good news today?

Remember how lovely it is to spend time with Him and how lovely it is when we bring good news to others.

27

The Blame Game

The next day he saw Jesus coming toward him, and said, "Behold, the Lamb of God, who takes away the sin of the world!"

John 1:29 (ESV)

*L*isten very carefully and we soon learn how good we are at blaming others and sidestepping responsibility for our actions. For example, we wouldn't lose our tempers if our co-workers were easier to get along with, or if our kids behaved better, or if our spouse were more considerate. Or, we would be very patient people if it weren't for traffic jams and long lines in the grocery store!

Let's rewind all the way back to the garden of Eden and meet Adam and Eve. In the third chapter of Genesis, God asks Adam the question:

"Have you eaten from the tree of which I commanded you that you should not eat?"

Genesis 3:11 (NKJV)

When God confronted him with his sin, Adam said:

"The woman whom you gave to be with me, she gave me fruit of the tree, and I ate."

Genesis 3:12 (NKJV)

From the very beginning, Adam tried to pawn off the responsibility for his sin: "The *woman* you gave me..." He shifted responsibility for his sin first to Eve – that she gave it to him – and then ultimately to God Himself, when he said, "The woman *you* gave me"! Adam did not accept personal responsibility for what he had done.

But the story still isn't over. God turns to Eve and asks her:

"What is this you have done?"

Genesis 3:13a (NKJV)

Listen to her answer:

"The serpent deceived me, and I ate."

Genesis 3:13b (NKJV)

Both of them were making excuses as a means of avoiding personal responsibility. If we play the blame game, we will always lose. As someone put it, "When people are lame, they love to blame." So what's the answer? Look again at the word 'blame' because the answer is hidden in it. If we shuffle the letters around, we can also make the word 'lamb'.

Read today's verse again. When the Lord Jesus came into the world, it was for the purpose of dealing with the issue of sin. Even though He was blameless, He took our sin upon Himself. He was born for you, He lived for you and He died for you. As Isaiah prophesied of Him:

But He was wounded for our transgressions,
He was bruised for our iniquities;
The chastisement for our peace was upon Him,
And by His stripes we are healed.
All we like sheep have gone astray;
We have turned, every one, to his own way;
And the LORD has laid on Him the iniquity of us all.

Isaiah 53:5-6 (NKJV)

Don't be lame and play the blame game. Accept what the Lamb of God has done for you. Don't focus on shifting the blame – focus on the Lamb; behold the Lamb of God.

28

Lend Me Your Ears

"Whatever He says to you, do it."

John 2:5 (NKJV)

"Friends, Romans, countrymen, lend me your ears" is the first line of a speech by Mark Antony in the play *Julius Caesar*, by William Shakespeare. Occurring in Act III, scene II, it is one of the most famous lines in all of Shakespeare's works.

"Lend me your ears." In other words, "Hear what I have to say." The Bible also invites us:

Give ear and hear my voice,
Listen and hear my speech.

Isaiah 28:23 (NKJV)

The Bible, however, goes a step further and asks us not just to hear but also to heed what is being said. Hearing and obeying are very closely related throughout the Bible. The New Testament word for 'hear' is *akouo*. The word for 'obey' is *hupakouo*, a compound word of two Greek words, *hupo* ('under') and *akouo* ('to hear'). Therefore, to obey is 'to hear under'. Obedience involves listening attentively with a heart of compliant submission and then acting on the word.

The message of hearing and obeying God's voice runs right through the Bible. Jesus said:

Therefore whoever hears these sayings of Mine, and does them, I will liken him to a wise man who built his house on the rock...

Matthew 7:24 (NKJV)

James tells us:

...be doers of the word, and not hearers only...

James 1:22 (NKJV)

Mary, the mother of Jesus, gave us one of the greatest summations of obedience:

"Whatever He says to you, do it."

John 2:5 (NKJV)

Obedience is simply doing whatever He says to do. Right at the heart of the great Commission we read the words "teaching them to obey".

'Therefore go and make disciples of all nations, baptising them in the name of the Father and of the Son and of the Holy Spirit, and teaching them to obey everything I have commanded you. And surely I am with you always, to the very end of the age.'

Matthew 28:19-20 (NIVUK)

Obeying Jesus and teaching others to obey Him is central to disciple-making.

Let's hear and heed the Word of God today.

29

Merely

But be doers of the Word [obey the message], and not merely listeners to it, betraying yourselves [into deception by reasoning contrary to the Truth].

James 1:22 (AMPC)

*D*oer: it's a word that has been popping up a lot recently in my daily readings. Am I merely a listener or an active doer? Am I internalising its meaning and actively obeying it? Another translation puts it:

Don't fool yourself into thinking that you are a listener when you are anything but, letting the Word go in one ear and out the other. Act on what you hear!

James 1:22 (MSG)

The same challenge arose in Luke 6:49:

But he who merely hears and does not practice doing My words is like a man who built a house on the ground without a foundation, against which the torrent burst, and immediately it collapsed and fell, and the breaking and ruin of that house was great.

Luke 6:49 (AMPC)

The word "merely" confronted me again as I glanced up the page in my Bible to Luke 6:32:

If you [merely] love those who love you, what quality of credit and thanks is that to you?

Luke 6:32 (AMPC)

Am I merely loving the lovable? Am I merely loving those who return love? Am I selective in whom I love? As a modern translation phrases it:

February

*If you only love the lovable, do you expect a pat on the back?
Run-of-the-mill sinners do that...*

Luke 6:32 (MSG)

And in a similar vein it appears in 1 John 3:18:

*Little children, let us not love [merely] in theory or in speech but
in deed and in truth (in practice and in sincerity).*

1 John 3:18 (AMPC)

Am I just talking about love or actually putting it into practice? As
the Living Bible puts it:

*Little children, let us stop just saying we love people; let us really
love them, and show it by our actions.*

1 John 3:18 (TLB)

Do not merely listen. Do not merely love.